STUDIES IN ENGLISH LITERATURE No. 2

General Editor

David Daiches

Professor of English in the School of English and American Studies,

University of Sussex

POPE: THE RAPE OF THE LOCK

by

J. S. CUNNINGHAM

Reader in English, University of York

EDWARD ARNOLD

First published 1961 by
Edward Arnold (Publishers) Ltd.
41 Maddox Street, London W1
Reprinted 1964
Reprinted 1967
Reprinted 1970

SBN 7131 5054 8 Cloth
SBN 7131 5055 6 Paper

Printed in Great Britain by Richard Clay (The Chaucer Press), Ltd.,
Bungay, Suffolk

General Preface

It has become increasingly clear in recent years that what both the advanced sixth former and the university student need most by way of help in their literary studies are close critical analyses and evaluations of individual works. Generalisations about periods or authors, general chat about the Augustan Age or the Romantic Movement, have their uses; but often they provide merely the illusion of knowledge and understanding of literature. All too often students come up to the university under the impression that what is required of them in their English literature courses is the referring of particular works to the appropriate generalisations about the writer or his period. Without taking up the anti-historical position of some of the American 'New Critics', we can nevertheless recognise the need for critical studies that concentrate on the work of literary art rather than on its historical background or cultural environment.

The present series is therefore designed to provide studies of individual plays, novels and groups of poems and essays, which are known to be widely studied in sixth forms and in universities. The emphasis is on clarification and evaluation; biographical and historical facts, while they may, of course, be referred to as helpful to an understanding of particular elements in a writer's work, will be subordinated to critical discussion. What kind of work is this? What exactly goes on here? How good is this work, and why? These are the questions which each writer will try to answer.

DAVID DAICHES

Acknowledgments

Professor Maynard Mack most generously read through my first four chapters as the book neared completion. I had already felt in his debt, as many must, for the stimulus provided by his essay ' "Wit and Poetry and Pope" '. I now have the added pleasure of thanking him for his close and helpful reading of my typescript.

To Professor Geoffrey Tillotson's edition of *The Rape of the Lock* in the Twickenham series I have been constantly indebted, for the information he makes compactly available to critics of the poem, and for the twin texts he most usefully provides.

I am grateful to the Durham Colleges Research Fund for readily assisting my visits to libraries during the preparation of the book.

My wife never lost patience with either the poem or the book, though repeatedly subjected to readings from both. This was invaluable help and encouragement.

J. S. C.

ABBREVIATIONS

Abbreviations used in the footnotes are explained
in the Bibliography (p. 63).

Contents

I desired that the Senate of *Rome* might appear before me in one large Chamber, and a modern Representative, in Counterview, in another. The first seemed to be an Assembly of Heroes and Demy-Gods; and other a Knot of Pedlars, Pick-Pockets, Highwaymen and Bullies.

> Swift, *Gulliver's Travels*, Book III, Ch. 7

O Vanity! how little is thy force acknowledged, or thy operations discerned! How wantonly dost thou deceive mankind under different disguises! Sometimes thou dost wear the face of pity, sometimes of generosity: nay, thou hast the assurance even to put on those glorious ornaments which belong only to heroic virtue.

> Fielding, *Joseph Andrews*, Ch. 15

My poem's epic, and is meant to be
    Divided in twelve books; each book containing,
With love, and war, a heavy gale at sea,
    A list of ships, and captains, and kings reigning,
New characters; the episodes are three:
    A panoramic view of hell's in training,
After the style of Virgil and of Homer,
So that my name of Epic's no misnomer.

> Byron, *Don Juan*, Canto I, stanza 20

1. Introductory

The ant's a centaur in his dragon world.
Pull down thy vanity, it is not man
Made courage, or made order, or made grace,
Pull down thy vanity, I say pull down.

Ezra Pound, *The Pisan Cantos*

'A poem on a slight subject requires the greatest care to make it considerable enough to be read.' When Pope made this remark to his friend Joseph Spence, he had (it seems) *The Dunciad* chiefly in mind; and recent criticism of that poem has dwelt on the meticulous and often furtive care with which Pope, while apparently preoccupied with the ephemera, the sweepings and nonentities of Grub Street and Fleet Ditch, attempts to persuade us of their paradoxical importance as symptoms of a widespread, perhaps irretrievable decline in civilised standards. The dunces act out their grossly comic *charade* on a stage which reverberates with mutilated hints, distorted echoes, of very 'considerable' things—classical epic, the Scriptures, Milton. As embodiments of the reductive will, defacers of the ideals these echoes call to mind, the dunces attain in the poem an unenviable significance far beyond their mere status in Pope's London. Conversely, as the posturing mimics of nobler figures, they are dwarfed by their own pretensions. This double activity of inflation and deflation, through which the dunces are at once below consideration *and* a serious menace, Pope achieves in so far as he contrives to expose the trivial by insinuation, allusion and parody—in so far as he 'implies and projects the possible other case, the case rich and edifying where the actuality is pretentious and vain'.[1]

'Slight is the subject.' This admission is made in the opening paragraph of *The Rape of the Lock*, and of course the poem is concerned—though not merely, nor simply—with a trivial episode. Lord Petre had snipped

[1] Henry James, 'The Lesson of the Master'. A fuller quotation is given on p. 59 below. An outstanding recent discussion of *The Dunciad* is Aubrey Williams, *Pope's 'Dunciad': A Study of its Meaning*, Methuen, 1955.

off a lock of Miss Arabella Fermor's hair, causing ill-feeling between their families. They had already, as it were, anticipated Pope by taking an amorous prank with extravagant seriousness. Pope outdoes them in absurdity, giving the incident full epic treatment. In other words, classical epic provides the 'rich and edifying' contrast against which the vanity and pretentiousness of the *beau monde* can be judged.

Even the admission of the triviality of the poem's 'subject'—

> Slight is the Subject, but not so the Praise,
> If She inspire, and He approve my Lays—

carries unsuspected weight: it echoes closely, and scales down, two lines from Virgil's fourth *Georgic*, which was itself much commended in Pope's time as the classical example of making mundane material 'considerable enough' by means of dignified treatment. Pope recalled Virgil's poem again in writing his Postscript to the translation of *The Odyssey*. His remarks fit *The Rape of the Lock* very neatly:

> Laughter implies censure; inanimate and irrational beings are not objects of censure; therefore these may be elevated as much as you please, and no ridicule follows, but when rational beings are represented above their real character, it becomes ridiculous in Art, as it is vicious in Morality. The *Bees* in *Virgil*, were they rational beings, would be ridiculous in having their actions and manners represented on a level with creatures so superior as men; since it would imply folly or pride, which are the proper objects of Ridicule.[1]

Belinda at the dressing-table's 'sacred Rites', the Baron building his altar of 'twelve vast *French* Romances', are caught in attitudes of comic seriousness. Representing them, as indeed they conceive of themselves, 'above their real character', coquette as goddess, philanderer as hero, the poem matches their moral failings with artistic absurdity.

The discrepancy between the world of heroic passions and conflicts, on the one hand, and the microcosm of modish *amours* and scandal, on the other, is firmly adumbrated from the start:

> What dire Offence from am'rous Causes springs,
> What mighty Contests rise from trivial Things. (i. 1–2)

This is, of course, the mock-heroic discrepancy. But we miss much of the joke unless we see how near true epic it is. The first line, while nicely

<hr />

[1] *Odyssey*, V. 299–300.

suited to Pope's poem, would also fit the passions roused by the rape of
Helen, or Agamemnon's seizure of Briseis from Achilles at the opening
of *The Iliad*. Then the phrase 'am'rous Causes', in the first line, modu-
lates into 'trivial Things' in the second. A slight change, masked by
rhythm and syntax: but it marks the shift from a possibly epic tension to
the full mock-epic discrepancy. The meeting of heroic and trivial in the
poem is as often a matter of such subtle transitions as of head-on col-
lision. And there *is* a sense in which even the 'mighty Contests . . .
trivial Things' discrepancy would fit classical epic: as Pope puts it, in the
playfully irreverent 'Dedication' to *The Rape*—'the ancient Poets are in
one respect like many modern Ladies; Let an Action be never so trivial
in it self, they always make it appear of the utmost Importance'. The
tone of this remark fits parts of the poem like a glove.[1]

But to say that *The Rape of the Lock* contrasts the mighty and the
trivial, to the ironic disparagement of the latter, is not enough, even if we
recognise how slight the shift from epic grandeur to mock-epic absurdity may be. We must not reduce to one set of terms a poem largely
distinguished, among mock-epics, by the variety of ironic contrasts on
which it draws. Along with 'mighty–trivial' we need other pairs of contraries—for instance, 'heroic–effete', 'primitive–sophisticated', 'antique–
contemporary', 'masculine–feminine', 'principled–opportunistic', 'dramatic–histrionic'. And although these contrasts work largely in favour
of 'the ancient Poets' and at the expense of 'modern Ladies', this is not
always the case. The gap between the contraries is very variable, from
the broadest burlesque of heroic ire in Sir Plume's bluster—

> Plague on't! 'tis past a Jest—nay prithee, Pox! (iv. 129)—

to Clarissa's rational appeal for sense and good humour, which in part
withstands comparison with its 'source', Sarpedon's ringing cry to battle
in *The Iliad* (Book XII). There are many times when one feels not so
much that Belinda's world is disparagingly contrasted with a more 'considerable', incomparably wider one, as that the world of Homer and
Virgil has been scaled down, wittily and affectionately, to admit the
boudoir and the coffee-table. In other words, the gap between the two

[1] Epic poets themselves are intermittently aware of the discrepancy.
Cf. the description of Satan in Chaos, *Paradise Lost*, ii. 920 ff.:

> Nor was his eare less peal'd
> With noises loud and ruinous (to compare
> Great things with small) than when *Bellona* storms

worlds can in this poem be ironically exploited to favour either side, or even both sides at once; it can remain more or less neutral, simply funny; and it can be closed, whether ludicrously, in that the Poets and the Ladies share a taste for ostentation, or seriously, in that Agamemnon—

> Till Time shall rifle ev'ry youthful Grace,
> And Age dismiss her from my cold Embrace (*Iliad*, i. 41–2)—

and Clarissa—

> But since, alas! frail Beauty must decay,
> Curl'd or uncurl'd, since Locks will turn to grey (v. 25–6)—

bow to a common denominator.

To some of the qualities of Belinda's world, and some of the values it respects, the poem itself bears witness, taking on the urbanity, polish and 'graceful Ease' which her society accomplished at its best. It is, to adopt a line of Pope's, 'Form'd to delight at once and lash the age' (*Epitaph on John Gay*). In the finesse of Pope's couplets is mirrored a cultivated dexterity and poise; his good-natured wit is a virtue of sophisticated, urbane conversation. It is true, of course, that these qualities are in part simply the mask for the poem's assault on a society preoccupied with the superficial, just as that society itself tended to disguise ugly realities under a prepossessing exterior. One of its earliest critics commented, shrewdly, 'Pope here appears in the light of a man of gallantry, and of a thorough knowledge of the world.'[1] If the poem assaults the *beau monde*, the attack is mostly good-humoured and tempered by a sense of the attractiveness of those whose failings are satirised, a sense of what delicacy, ceremony and elegance could mean at best.

Its delicacy is the most engaging feature of Belinda's world. What she prizes glitters as only the ephemeral and the exquisite can. Her moment of gracefulness, beauty and universal conquest is penultimate. The poise her society so prizes is nourished by tension—and here again the poem mirrors as well as criticises, in the perpetual interplay of poise and tension in Pope's couplets. In the recognition of this fragility, the necessary frailty and transience of the beautiful, the gap between heroic and non-heroic is closed. The epic omens foreshadowing the loss of Belinda's curls are not entirely hollow, the epic laments over human impermanence are poignant in this context as in Homer. Pope is not merely setting the loss of a mere lock of hair in ironic perspective through the mock-heroic

[1] Joseph Warton, *Essay on the Writings and Genius of Pope*, 1756, p. 246.

mechanism: he is, paradoxically, touching it with seriousness. In this poem the transience of the ephemeral is moving. The 'mighty Contests' are not mighty; but the loss of the lock is not simply a 'trivial Thing'.

This all amounts to noticing once again, as a reader of the poem can hardly fail to notice, that it runs, with a self-delighting dexterity, through a wide range of attitudes, commanding a startling variety of tones. These features should emerge in analysis. In the meantime, it is important to recognise the essential complexity—in some cases, the ambivalence—of Pope's attitudes to the contrasted worlds of Homer and Belinda. His attitudes to classical epic are partly conditioned by, partly independent of, his reading of Homer's commentators and critics. His attitudes to the *beau monde* are formed partly from observation, partly from the critiques already offered by the Restoration dramatists and the periodical essayists. Both worlds had, for Pope and his audience, special defining characteristics. As a translator of Homer, Pope turned to his purpose the special 'heroick' idiom which he found best exemplified in Dryden's *Aeneid*. As a critic of Homer, he used the special set of terms accepted for the discussion of epic—as the 'Dedication' slyly puts it, 'The *Machinery*, Madam, is a Term invented by the Criticks.' As a portrayer of upper-class manners, he used the anatomised figures (prude, rake and coquette) and the modish language ('*Wounds*, *Charms*, and *Ardors*') already familiar to readers and theatre-goers as contemporary 'types' and current absurdities.

These are only a few elements in, so to speak, the 'significant soil' which nourishes that vigorous and, in the end, independent plant, the poem. *The Rape of the Lock*, though deeply rooted in its own time, can be read and enjoyed with comparatively little explanatory annotation; but full understanding can be built up only from a sense of the unique moment in which it occurs. It is a moment of great interest in the course of neo-classicism, and in the history of the epic itself. Here is a mock-epic written by a poet who had an ambition to write an epic of his own, and whose translation of *The Iliad* has recently been called 'the last non-satiric poem of the European heroic tradition'.[1] It is a complex, precarious moment, a point of intersection for a whole web of attitudes and sympathies.

This is, then, a perpetually surprising poem, a trap for those who label it or who treat it consistently seriously or with consistent levity. It asks of its reader a continuous alert responsiveness: a readiness to laugh on one

[1] Knight, p. 107.

page at Sir Fopling's operatic *cliché* '*Those Eyes are made so killing*' (v. 64), while catching the element of serious homage in Pope's reference to 'all the Murders' of Belinda's eyes (v. 145); a willingness to be startled by the sudden irruption into the prevailing tone of exuberant, urbane mockery, of something far more astringent—

> The hungry Judges soon the Sentence sign,
> And Wretches hang that Jury-men may dine. (iii. 21–2)

An irrepressible *jeu d'esprit*, the poem is also a serious anatomy of 'polite' behaviour, and probes the ageless hurts and pretences of the sex war. A mimicry of epic that would have delighted Martin Scriblerus, it draws on an intimate knowledge of, and full sympathy with, the Renaissance epic ideal. Above all, this is the mock-epic of a mock-world, the make-believe celebration of a society of play-actors. In Belinda's charmed microcosm, where the privileged carry on the masquerade of social ritual and intrigue, there are no worse penalties than prolonged spinster-hood or loss of 'face'. What *they* think—'the horrid things they say' (iv. 108)—sways action much more easily than a sense of principle or honour. Honour itself has dwindled to mean mere reputation.

And yet Pope makes the predicament Belinda finds herself in, and the penalties she dreads, vividly present to our imaginative sympathy. Observing with dispassion, we are also compelled to respond with feeling intelligence. Some of the poem's hyperboles are neither humorous nor satiric, but sincere. And if an ironic innuendo undercuts a compliment, there is nevertheless a level on which the compliment engagingly survives:

> If to her share some Female Errors fall,
> Look on her Face, and you'll forget 'em all. (ii. 17–18)

This couplet is also a nice example of Pope's adroitness as a reviser of his own work: its fine balance was achieved only when he substituted the milder word 'forget' for the outright 'forgive' of the early version. Forgiveness was too much to promise, even in jest.

2. *Ancient Poets*

Thence form your Judgment, thence your Maxims bring,
And trace the Muses upward to their Spring.
Essay on Criticism, 126–7

At no stage in his career would Pope have doubted that this couplet on Homer carried an indispensable piece of advice for poet and critic alike. To learn from Homer, as Virgil and (at its best) the epic tradition since him had learnt, was not simply to follow the rule-book, which Pope had a healthy distrust of, with its 'dull receipts how poems may be made'. It was to emulate a great original, whose stride seemed to take in the whole range of basic human impulses and feelings and predicaments, one who wrote, with an almost unfailing discretion, in a heroic idiom for which no less a poet than Dryden had tried to develop an English equivalent. From Homer, ultimately, the whole living classical tradition derived its network of principles, assumptions, conventions—and 'rules'.

On the active strength of that tradition *The Rape of the Lock*, no less than Pope's translations of Homer, depends. An allegiance which could hold a poet to more than twelve years of labour in acclimatising Homer to English ears was easily robust enough to withstand its own self-mockery. At the same time, Pope had to reckon, as critic and translator, and above all as an original poet working within a vigorous tradition, with a sense of the distance stretching between his society, his thinking, his language, and those of Homer and Virgil—or even Milton. Pope's sense of this gap is, alternately, a challenge to the translator, 'attempting to write as Homer would if he were an eighteenth-century English poet',[1] a cause of some embarrassment to the critic, and a source of ironic contrast to the poet. Each aspect links up with the others. For instance, the translator's 'heroick' idiom, which partly emphasises the elevation and antiquity of epic and partly adapts epic to the eighteenth-century audience, finds its more violent complement in the mock-epic poet's yoking together of the ancient and the contemporary; or, again, the embarrassment felt by the critic in discussing Homer's gods (after Hobbes and Locke!) prompts the poet to toy with them affectionately, with a sense of their primitive power, or to substitute deities of his own

[1] Brower, p. 115.

invention which need not be taken seriously either in themselves or as a parody of Homer.

Mock-heroic was, then, an invaluable tactic for Pope. It turned to account his embarrassment with some features of epic itself and of the epic tradition—not to mention the innumerable pedants and critics—by deliberately emphasising it in a humorous context. It solved the problem of how to give a modern, comparatively trivial subject elevated treatment, simply by forcing ancient and modern into uncomfortable proximity. If the modern world resists epic treatment, then mock-heroic makes this very resistance prominent, insinuating a current shortage of the proper heroic material—'this "epic" poem is absurd because there are not enough heroes to write about nowadays'. If the urge to write serious epic is daunted by the size of the undertaking and by the pressure of ponderous critical advice on how to go about it, then mock-heroic can simultaneously appease the ambition and mock the prescribers by following all their precepts except the crucial one—dignity of subject. Mock-epic does no great disservice to the epic tradition, while making no concession to it that might embarrass eighteenth-century rationality.

The 'background' to mock-epic in Pope is a situation of some intricacy, full of ironic potential and stimulus for wit. Admiration for epic is tempered by a sense of its remoteness: the 'Heathen Divinities', Pope himself remarked, were now 'not open enough to the understanding'.[1] And if, on the one hand, Pope could write

> Learn hence for Ancient Rules a just esteem;
> To copy Nature is to copy them,

he could also declare

> I am sawcy enough to think that one may sometimes differ from *Aristotle* without blundering, and . . . I am sure one may sometimes fall into an error by following him servilely.[2]

Nature and Homer

In commenting on the description of Thersites in *The Iliad*, Book II, Pope writes: 'whether ludicrous Descriptions ought to have a Place in the *Epic* Poem, has been justly question'd'.[3] The note is both perfectly

[1] Letter to Bolingbroke, 9 April 1724. *Correspondence*, ii. 228.

[2] The couplet is from *Essay on Criticism*, 139–40. The prose is from *Odyssey*, V. 314.

[3] *Iliad*, I. 155.

comprehensible and oddly inconsistent. Pope is testing Homer by the standard of *decorum* which is, of course, of the first importance in eighteenth-century poetry and literary theory, related as it is, through the sense of what is 'natural' and 'proper' (two words which frequently, in this context, amount to the same thing), to classical precept and precedent as well as to the prized common sense of how men behaved (Johnson's 'general properties and large appearances'). A more versatile principle than *decorum* would be hard to find. In its light, not only could the tone of a description be questioned on critical grounds, as the ideal conception of epic excluded the ludicrous, but a hero's conduct could be questioned on grounds of morality and class, as epic ought to exclude behaviour associated with 'low life'. Rapin, for instance, had been disturbed to find that 'In Homer, Kings and Princes speak as scurrilously one of another as Porters would do', and had been driven to regret that 'there is but little observance of Decorum in *Homers* poems: Fathers are therein harsh and cruell, the Heroes weak and passionate, the Gods subject to miseries, unquiet, quarrelsome, and not enduring one another'.[1] Such a judgment, though understandable enough in the light of neo-classical argument from *decorum*, aptly illustrates the absurd extremes to which the argument could be pushed. The wheel comes full circle in the arraignment of Homer by a standard itself derived, however deviously and wishfully, from his own poems. Pope himself took issue with Rapin on this score, commenting

> methinks the *French* Criticks play double with us, when they sometimes represent the Rules of Poetry to be form'd upon the Practice of *Homer*, and at other times arraign their Master as if he transgress'd them.[2]

This is a sensible protest against the argumentative tangles into which neo-classicism could all too easily fall. But logically it also rules out Pope's objection to the ludicrous description of Thersites. There are, of course, ways out of the thicket: had Pope been challenged on this issue, he might have replied that this was an uncharacteristic lapse on Homer's part, the kind of thing never found in Virgil; or he might have had second thoughts, and justified Homer on the grounds that he was 'imitating Nature' as it was in his time, this being a line of reasoning familiar to critics of Homer. But the discussion would be little clearer, in effect, for all the familiarity of its terms. For one thing, it would have

[1] Rapin, p. 56.   [2] *Iliad*, I. 51.

B

fallen into the common error of using 'Nature' in one sense (observed reality) to excuse what, applying a different sense of the same word (correctness), is judged a fault.

In translating Homer, Pope was repeatedly confronted with problems raised by his orthodox assumptions concerning the sublimity of epic and the need for a sustained grandeur in the heroic idiom. As early as 1710, he argues that Dryden's *Aeneid* was at fault in using nautical jargon, on the principle that 'no Terms of Art, or Cant-Words, suit with the Majesty & Dignity of Style which Epic Poetry requires'.[1] The complement to this criticism is found, years later, in Pope's Postscript to his translation of *The Odyssey*, where he observes how difficult it is to imitate Homer in the 'lower parts'—'For it is as hard for an Epic Poem to stoop to the Narrative with success, as for a Prince to descend to be familiar, without diminution to his greatness'.[2] Homer himself needed making more 'poetical' by his translator, 'in order to dignify and solemnize these plainer parts, which hardly admit of any poetical ornaments'.[3] For this reason, Pope explains, he used some Miltonic phrases in *The Odyssey*, to make the style look 'judiciously antiquated'. The prejudice against all but the grandest language for the writing or translation of epic survived in criticism long after Pope. In 1776 James Beattie presses it even further, objecting to the use of jargon and oaths 'even in the *Mock-heroic*, except perhaps in a short characteristical speech, like that of Sir Plume in the *Rape of the Lock*'.[4]

The consequences of the traditional insistence on *decorum* in the language of epic are of importance for the reader of mock-epic too. For one thing, it pointed the joke, sharpened the shock-value, of a reversal of propriety so conspicuous as, say, the description of a society lady in terms that would suit the arming of Achilles: as Pope himself put it,

> the use of the grand style on little subjects, is not only ludicrous, but a sort of transgression against the rules of proportion and mechanicks: 'Tis using a vast force to lift a *feather*.[5]

This is exactly the reverse of what the intending epic poet is advised to do in *The Art of Sinking in Poetry*:

> It is also useful to employ *Technical Terms*, which estrange your Stile from the great and general Ideas of Nature: And the higher your

---

[1] Letter to Henry Cromwell, 28 October 1710. *Correspondence*, i. 101.
[2] *Odyssey*, V. 302. [3] *Odyssey*, V. 304.
[4] *Essays*, 1776, p. 407. [5] *Odyssey*, V. 299.

Subject is, the lower should you search into Mechanicks for your Expression. If you describe the Garment of an Angel, say that his *Linnen* was *finely spun*, and *bleach'd on the happy Plains*. Call an Army of Angels, *Angelic Cuirassiers*.[1]

The examples of bathos used here are taken, we are informed, from 'the English Homer', poor Sir Richard Blackmore; and the joke is complete when Pope achieves a similar lapse from the expected grand periphrasis, describing the diminutive gods of *The Rape of the Lock* as 'The light *Militia* of the lower Sky' (i. 42). In that the sylphs are parodies of epic deities, the phrase is bathetic, an offence against the *decorum* of the high style; in that they are ineffectual, the phrase is comically flattering— though, like the militia, they are certainly 'light'!

The many lines in the poem which would not look out of place in true epic—lines anticipating or echoing Pope's Homer, or mimicking such precursors as Dryden's *Aeneid*—stand, therefore, in the bleakest possible contrast with the non-epic material and with the absurd lapses from heightened language. Given its obligatory sustained elevation, any change from the heroic pitch is likely to be felt as an anti-climax. To the eighteenth-century reader, at least, the transition from

> Mean while declining from the Noon of Day,
> The Sun obliquely shoots his burning Ray (iii. 19–20)

to

> The Merchant from th'*Exchange* returns in Peace,
> And the long Labours of the *Toilette* cease (iii. 23–4)

is a startling lapse from grand generality to trivial particulars, even if he missed the straightforward allusion to *The Odyssey* in the first of these couplets, and in the last line the distorted echo of a line quoted by Dryden's Aeneas from Anchises:

> And the long Labours of your Voyage end. (*Aeneid*, vii. 171)

Again and again *The Rape of the Lock* gears the reader's response to the full epic generality and grandeur, touching off chain reactions of association with Dryden, Milton, Virgil, Homer, only to slip back nonchalantly into the prosaic or the specific—or the other way round. Thus, the thoroughly traditional opening couplet of the second canto heralds (merely) a description of Belinda on the Thames, with a pomp

[1] *The Art of Sinking in Poetry*, ed. E. L. Steeves, New York, 1952, p. 62.

reserved for Aeneas on the Tiber; or, to reverse the process, the end of the same canto caps the description of the sylphs' panicky flutterings with a sonorous epic formula:

> With beating Hearts the dire Event they wait,
> Anxious, and trembling for the Birth of Fate. (ii. 141–2)

These switches in and out of the epic world and the heroic style are, of course, characteristic of mock-epic; but few mock-heroic poets are able to accomplish them with such dexterity, barely disturbing the surface grooming of the couplets. Crossing the gap again and again, Pope manages to pretend that it is not really there, as in some respects it is not.

But in explaining mock-heroic's conspicuous reversal of *decorum*, we must not overlook another aspect of the matter. In 1753, Joseph Warton, who was to become one of Pope's earliest full-scale critics, wrote:

> The tea and card tables can be introduced with propriety and success only in the mock-heroic . . . but the present modes of life must be forgotten when we attempt anything in the serious or sublime poetry; for heroism disdains the luxurious refinements, the false delicacy and state of modern ages.
>
> The primeval, I was about to say, patriarchal simplicity of manners displayed in the ODYSSEY, is a perpetual source of true poetry, and in-expressibly pleasing to all who are uncorrupted by the business and vanity of life.[1]

Society life is below the dignity of all poetry except mock-heroic; modern life in general is too corrupt to afford material for serious poets. Warton's terms suggest the myth of the Golden Age, and the analogy with the pastoral mechanism is clear: rustics are allowed into pastoral only on the best behaviour consistent with remaining 'primitive', whereas the behaviour of a modern lord is hardly noble enough for 'primitive' heroic treatment. Warton's moralistic reading of the ancient–modern contrast here is by no means unusual in Homer criticism, and it is, need-less to say, of the first importance for an understanding of mock-epic. Reading the contrast morally was no doubt encouraged by the orthodox critical emphasis on the *moral* of an epic poem. Dryden had been content to defer to authority on this question, remarking in 1679, 'The first rule which Bossu prescribes to the writer of an Heroic Poem . . . is to make the moral of the work.'[2] Pope took the prescription seriously enough

---

[1] *The Adventurer*, no. lxxx, 11 August 1753.

[2] Dryden, *Essays*, ed. Ker, i. 213.

to take care, as *The Rape of the Lock* developed towards its final form, to see that it satisfied the critics in this particular.[1]

The morality of the contrast between Homer's world and Belinda's could be read either way, and critics of Homer had, as Pope saw, 'generally carry'd into Extreams' one or other side of the argument.[2] On the one hand, it could be asserted, with Joseph Warton, that Homer's world was much nobler (and hence more amenable to 'poetical' treatment) than its sorry modern counterpart. Mme Dacier puts the point conveniently for us:

> Is it possible for those who are now-a-days used to our Romantic Heroes, those Court-Heroes, always so nice, so whining, and so polite, to endure *Achilles, Patroclus, Agamemnon* and *Ulysses*, busy'd in what we call servile Offices?[3]

On the other hand, Rapin could argue that Homer's world was barbaric:

> In fine, this Hero of *Homer* [Achilles], whose repute is so great, and so highly celebrated through all ages, is but an epitome of imperfections and vices.[4]

Pope knew and respected these and other critics of Homer, and on this question of the moral contrast between ancient and modern he is aware of the traditional embarrassments. Homer's heroes, as he puts it, have 'vicious and *imperfect Manners*'.[5] His notes to the translation of *The Iliad* show him taking now one side, now the other. He can comment admiringly on the epic feast as a demonstration of 'the wonderful Simplicity of the old heroic Ages', yet be troubled by Agamemnon's ruthlessness in battle, seeing it as morally offensive.[6]

The dilemma is genuine and deep-seated, and Pope is no less orthodox (and muddled) than many of his predecessors in seeking a way out of it. In the Preface to *The Iliad* he at first disagrees with Mme Dacier's praise of the manners of the epic world:

> Who can be so prejudiced in their Favour as to magnify the Felicity of those Ages, when a Spirit of Revenge and Cruelty reign'd thro' the World, when no Mercy was shown but for the sake of Lucre, when

[1] See p. 23 below.
[2] *Iliad* (Preface), I. fol. D3.
[3] Dacier, I. iv.
[4] Rapin, p. 22.
[5] *Iliad* (Preface), I. fol. D3.
[6] *Iliad*, II. 577 and II. 490.

the greatest Princes were put to the Sword, and their Wives and Daughters made Slaves and Concubines? [1]

Such a view sorts ill with the established notions of heroic nobility. The compromise Pope offers, as did Rapin before him, is to treat Homer as documentary, ascribing the 'immorality' of his heroes 'to the uncivilized Manners of those Times, when Mankind was not united by the Bonds of a rational Society'.[2] Homer, alas, knew nothing of John Locke or Parliamentary government. Yet even here lingers the pastoral prejudice in favour of the Golden Age, before the advent of luxury and class-distinction:

> There is a Pleasure in taking a view of that Simplicity in Opposition to the Luxury of succeeding Ages; in beholding Monarchs without their Guards, Princes tending their Flocks, and Princesses drawing Water from the Springs.[3]

Against such a background of rather confused discussion *The Rape of the Lock* should be seen. Dr. Johnson praised Pope's translation of *The Iliad* for toning down Homer's 'barbarity', and remarked that 'A hero would wish to be loved as well as to be reverenced.' [4] A recent critic, similarly, has traced Pope's alteration of the Homeric hero, in his translation, into a figure more adapted to the eighteenth-century reader's sense of 'how a noble lord behaved, how he walked and how he talked on great occasions':

> A chief or a prince in council could not quarrel like a fishwife, as Achilles and Agamemnon seemed to in any literal translation of their speeches.[5]

In Pope's translation of the great Sarpedon speech, the habits of mind of a Homeric hero have, it is argued, been turned into those of 'a contemporary reader of the *Essay on Man*'.[6] The 'parody' of the same speech in *The Rape of the Lock*, put into the mouth of Clarissa in the 1717

[1] *Iliad* (Preface), I. fol. D3.

[2] *Iliad*, II. 490.

[3] *Iliad* (Preface), I. fol. D3ᵛ. Cf. Dacier, I. xxii: 'I am pleas'd to see *Juno* dress herself, without that Train of Toilette, Chamber-Maid, Tire-Woman.' As Pope said elsewhere (*Iliad*, V. 1106): 'One may preach till Doomsday on this Subject, but all the Commentators in the World will never prevail upon a Lady to stick one Pin the less in her Gown . . .'

[4] *Lives*, iii. 239.   [5] Brower, p. 106.   [6] Brower, p. 111.

revision, shows the same process, except that it has become self-conscious and ironically weighted. The heroic ideal of clear-sighted action based on a full reckoning of the cost is represented, in Clarissa's words, as simultaneously degraded into mere worldliness and moral opportunism *and* modulated into an attitude different from the heroic but by no means ridiculous, and confronting some of the same misfortunes as Sarpedon: 'Disease, and Death's inexorable Doom'.

The heroes in Belinda's world are puny caricatures of an Achilles or a Sarpedon; but at best, Pope implies, this society ought to exact conduct based on principles no less mature than the heroic, and perhaps more enlightened and civilized. However prominent the heroic ideals may be as the magnifying glass through which the fops' imperfections and the ladies' vanity are seen, they cannot simply be taken over entire into a world of different standards, different conflicts and penalties. The main point is that the simultaneous double aspect of Clarissa's speech is a counterpart of the double attitude taken by Pope in his criticism to the question of heroic barbarity.

Pope introduced Clarissa's speech, Warburton remarked, 'to open more clearly the MORAL of the Poem'.[1] He was, of course, aware that a 'moral' was thought by the critics to be essential to epic, and he himself made no bones about summarising the 'moral' of *The Iliad*—namely, 'that Concord, among Governours, is the preservation of States, and Discord the ruin of them'.[2] From its inception, *The Rape of the Lock* had a moral motivation, teaching the lesson of concord and good humour to the quarrelling families. Pope's 'Dedication' had delicately indicated the moral implications, or at least the less severe ones, of his satire on high society: the poem was, he says, 'intended only to divert a few young Ladies, who have good Sense and good Humour enough, to laugh not only at their Sex's little unguarded Follies, but at their own'. For all that, a critic as dogmatic, and as antagonistic, as John Dennis could find the poem lacking in 'moral' by the strictest classical standards. Arguing that the poem had no 'moral' to offer, Dennis chose in contrast to summarise the teaching of Boileau's mock-epic *Le Lutrin*:

The Moral is, *That when Christians, and especially the Clergy, run into great Heats about religious Trifles, their Animosity proceeds from the Want of that Religion which is their Pretence of the Quarrel.*[3]

[1] See Twickenham edition, p. 195.
[2] *Iliad*, VI. fol. II H.
[3] See Twickenham edition, pp. 368 ff.

In his own copy of Dennis's remarks, Pope altered this summary in such a way as to show that it could easily be made to fit his own poem, if for 'Clergy' we read 'Ladies', and for 'Religion' we read 'sense'. He underlined Dennis's adjective 'religious', indicating perhaps the pseudo-devotional fervour with which Belinda applies cosmetics, or the exaggerated sanctity attached to the lock of hair. At any rate, he concedes the relevance to mock-heroic of the traditional demand for a 'moral', and is complimented by Johnson for observing it:

> Perhaps neither Pope nor Boileau has made the world much better than he found it; but if they had both succeeded, it were easy to tell who would have deserved most from publick gratitude. The freaks, and humours, and spleen, and vanity of women, as they embroil families in discord and fill houses with disquiet, do more to obstruct the happiness of life in a year than the ambition of the clergy in many centuries.[1]

Johnson has, for the moment, lost his sense of the poem's lightness of touch, and in consequence he over-weights his account of its moral implications. But there need be no question that they are in the poem for the taking, though at varying levels of suppression, and with varying degrees of severity.

'The *Machinery*, Madam, is a Term invented by the Criticks, to signify that Part which the Deities, Angels, or Dæmons, are made to act in a Poem' (Pope's Dedication). The Machines, no less than a 'moral', were accounted indispensable to epic by the orthodox critics, as Pope was well aware. He also knew that the use of the supernatural in classical epic was a major source of embarrassment to the modern commentator, as well as a daunting obstacle to the production of an original epic poem in modern times. 'The heathen deities,' Johnson remarked, 'can no longer gain attention.'[2] Addison, reviewing the volume of poems in which *The Rape of the Lock* first appeared, was no less emphatic: 'for a Christian author to write in the pagan creed, to make prince Eugene a favourite of Mars, or to carry on a correspondence between Bellona and the marshal de Villars, would be downright puerility, and unpardonable in a poet that is past sixteen'.[3] Dryden had conceded the necessity of supernatural agency in epic, and had reflected discouragingly on the feebleness of 'the

---

[1] *Lives*, iii. 234.

[2] *Lives*, iii.233.

[3] *The Spectator*, no. 523, 30 October 1712.

machines of our Christian religion' for such a purpose.[1] If this was so, and if, as Dryden thought, no Christian author should introduce 'heathen deities' into his poem, then the would-be writer of epic was faced with an unattractive choice between the use of doctrinally acceptable but (*pace* Milton) poetically chilling immortals, on the one hand, and the hazard of inventing Machines of his own, on the other.

Pope was confronted with this amusingly rational embarrassment over Machines, both in translating Homer and in trying to make *The Rape of the Lock*, as part of the joke, meet the critics' requirements for epic in this respect as in others. In *The Iliad* he attempts to make the Homeric gods comprehensible, and even acceptable, to an audience which would expect consistency, and which would be pacified by being encouraged to look at Zeus with a philosophic eye accustomed to the tidier universe of Milton or Virgil. In *The Rape* a magnificent inventive stroke despatches the pagan gods to virtual oblivion and substitutes, along with the paraphernalia of Fate and Love (far too ponderous, by design, for this context), regiments of airborne waifs and strays who are the barely tangible images of feminine delicacy and also carry much of the poem's satire of the fair sex's 'little unguarded Follies'. Thus, at one blow Pope contrives to satisfy critical precept and to circumvent the awkwardness over epic Machines by inventing deities exquisitely adapted to his needs. Johnson, following Dennis, thought them too little 'intermingled with the action'.[2] But their very ineffectiveness is vital to the poem.

Imitators and Pedants

> Some on the Leaves of ancient Authors prey,
> Nor Time nor Moths e'er spoiled as much as they;
> Some drily plain, without Invention's Aid,
> Write dull Receipts how Poems may be made;
> These leave the Sense, their Learning to display,
> And those explain the Meaning quite away.
>
> *Essay on Criticism*, 112–17

Pope knew only too well that to 'trace the Muses upward to their spring' was much easier said than done, and that much of the intervening country was monotonous and choked with undergrowth. To give an account of the development of learned commentary on Homer was itself a tall order, a matter of trying 'to make something out of a hundred

---

[1] *Essays*, ed. Ker, ii. 32.   [2] *Lives*, iii. 235.

Pedants that is not Pedantical'.[1] Like the pedants, the imitators of Homer had, from Virgil onwards, slavishly followed in the same track:

> If *Ulysses* visit the Shades, the *Æneas* of *Virgil* and *Scipio* of *Silius* are sent after him. If he be detain'd from his Return by the Allurements of *Calypso*, so is *Æneas* by *Dido*, and *Rinaldo* by *Armida*. If *Achilles* be absent from the *Army* on the Score of a Quarrel thro' half the Poem, *Rinaldo* must absent himself just as long, on the like account.[2]

Eventually a point is reached at which this whole vast expense of energy, by poets and pedants alike, looks more ludicrous than diverting—a point of frustration when prescriptions for the writing of epic have become multiple and stereotyped, and when the effort to abide by them has exhausted the inventive capacity which might, given latitude, have discovered 'noble Morals told in a new Variety of Accidents'.[3] At such a point the cleavage between a dull, plodding classicism of the letter and the enlightened, vigorous classicism of the spirit is at its sharpest. The mockery of solemn pedantic irrelevance, in the tradition of *A Tale of a Tub*, catches the fashion among the wits. The primacy of the epic form, the coherence of the major heroic tradition, the vitality of epic poetry as a permanent ideal, both moral and literary—none of these notions is yet seriously weakened; but 'the declining State of *Heroick Poetry* in our times' is giving concern,[4] and there seems to be no way of keeping it respectably alive, unless by way of translation from the classics.

At this moment the intending epic poet would ponder Dryden's twice-repeated claim that 'an Heroic Poem is certainly the greatest work of human nature'.[5] He would hear himself required to exhibit 'besides an universal genius . . . universal learning', and be told—not by Dryden alone—that

> he must have exactly studied Homer and Virgil as his patterns; Aristotle and Horace as his guides; Vida and Bossu as their commentators; with many others, both Italian and French critics, which I want leisure here to recommend.[6]

Pope told Spence that he himself would have attempted to write an original epic, had he not turned to the translating of Homer. We may

---

[1] *Iliad*, I. 48.   [2] *Iliad* (Preface), I. fol. B4.   [3] *Iliad*, I. 49.

[4] *Monsieur Bossu's Treatise of the Epick Poem*, London, 1695, fol. a8 ('Preface of the Translator').

[5] *Essays*, ed. Ker, ii. 43 and ii. 154.   [6] *Essays*, ed. Ker, ii. 43.

wonder if, in the circumstances, there was not a sense of relief in taking even so arduous an alternative. Pope could, after all, remember trying his hand at epic—admittedly, at a very early age—and finding how tempting it was to let 'imitation' hinder 'invention'. Describing his abandoned juvenile effort to Spence, he said

> I endeavoured in this poem to collect all the beauties of the great epic writers into one piece: there was Milton's style in one part, and Cowley's in another; here the style of Spenser imitated, and there of Statius; here Homer and Virgil, and there Ovid and Claudian. . . . It was better planned than Blackmore's Prince Arthur; but as slavish an imitation of the ancients.[1]

In 1712 and thereabouts Pope makes three vigorous responses to the moment of frustration at which the epic tradition had arrived: he takes up the translation of Homer, writes *The Rape of the Lock* and produces a whimsically pungent essay, 'A Receit to Make an Epic Poem'. In this essay, Pope satirises pedants and poetasters alike, by pushing into nonchalant absurdity the worst tendencies of both.[2] He begins by re-iterating the praise of epic as 'the greatest work Human Nature is capable of', and the main orthodox requirements of the epic poet—'a Genius', 'to be knowing in all Arts and Sciences', and 'a Compleat Skill in Languages'. Then he sets out, with Swiftian aplomb, 'to make it manifest, that Epick Poems may be made *without a Genius*, nay without Learning or much Reading'. There follow absurd instructions for making an epic out of, so to speak, a collection of spare parts—the poetaster's do-it-yourself kit, comprising the Fable, the Manners, the Machines, the Descriptions and the Language. This does not amount to a thorough-going repudiation of the critics of epic, even at their most prescriptive in Le Bossu. But it *is* a satirical commentary on the direction in which they pointed, as well as a witty oblique gloss on what Pope was doing in *The Rape of the Lock*.

The essay reduces epic, as the critics tended to, from a living organism to an assemblage of items. To make an epic fable, Pope advises,

> Take out of any old Poem, History-books, Romance, or Legend, (for instance Geffry of Monmouth or Don Belianis of Greece) those Parts of

---

[1] Spence, pp. 47–8, 50.

[2] First published in *The Guardian*, no. 78, 10 June 1713. Reprinted in *Prose Works of Alexander Pope*, ed. N. Ault, 1936, p. 115.

*Story which afford most Scope for long Descriptions: Put these Pieces to-
gether, and throw all the Adventures you fancy into one Tale. Then take a
Hero, whom you may chuse for the Sound of his Name, and put him into the
midst of these Adventures: There let him work, for twelve Books; at the end
of which you may take him out, ready prepared to conquer or to marry; it
being necessary that the Conclusion of an Epick Poem be fortunate.*

The Hero is a mere collection of 'all the best Qualities you can find in all
the best celebrated Heroes of Antiquity', and an epic battle may be
described by the theft of 'a large quantity of Images and Similes from
Homer's Iliads, with a Spice or two of Virgil'. The Language can
acquire the 'venerable Air of Antiquity' (anticipating the 'venerable air',
the 'style judiciously antiquated', which Pope sought in translating *The
Odyssey* [1]), by 'darkening it up and down with *Old English*'. And the
notorious difficulty over the Machines is nonchalantly ignored by re-
commending a random assortment of Gods:

> *Take of Deities, Male and Female, as many as you can use. Separate
> them into two equal parts, and keep Jupiter in the middle. Let Juno put him
> in a Ferment, and Venus mollifie him. Remember on all Occasions to make
> use of Volatile Mercury. If you have need of Devils, draw them out of
> Milton's Paradise, and extract your Spirits from Tasso.*

Here, as in *The Rape of the Lock*, one senses Pope's relief in turning admiration momentarily into hilarious irreverence. On one view, indeed,
the poem might be taken as a delighted demonstration of how to make
an epic poem out of virtually nothing, according to some such recipe.
But it is also far more than that. It attains an imaginative coherence of its
own, for all its dependence on eclectic allusiveness and the fragmentation
of epic.

In his Preface to *The Iliad*, Pope retains the established critical cate-
gories—Fable, Characters, Sentiments and so on—but keeps in view the
point which the 'Receit' had satirically underlined. Homer's powers of
construction, his artistic sense, are one thing, the imaginative grasp and
inventiveness another:

> Exact Disposition, just Thought, correct Elocution, polish'd
> Numbers, may have been found in a thousand; but this *Poetical Fire*,
> this *Vivida vis animi*, in a very few.[2]

[1] *Odyssey*, V. 304. ('And let our love to Antiquity be ever so great, a
fine ruin is one thing, and a heap of rubbish another').

[2] *Iliad* (Preface), I. fol. B2ᵛ.

The point is not new—Mme Dacier had praised Homer for 'the Fire and the Soul he puts into his Words' [1]—but Pope makes it repeatedly, and with obvious conviction. Here is the 'grace beyond the reach of art' which, as Pope says, 'can over-power Criticism, and make us admire even while we dis-approve'.[2]

Much the same point, on a smaller scale, needs making for *The Rape of the Lock*. It obeys all the 'rules', in a context of affectionate mockery. But it is also, in its turn, touched by an imaginative fire which can hardly be accounted for by describing it simply as a 'mock-epic'. Joseph Warton was prompted to call it 'the truest and liveliest picture of modern life',[3] and Dr. Johnson praised its powers of imaginative discovery and re-creation:

> new things are made familiar, and familiar things are made new. A race of aerial people never heard of before is presented to us in a manner so clear and easy, that the reader seeks for no further information, but immediately mingles with his new acquaintance, adopts their interests and attends their pursuits, loves a sylph and detests a gnome.
>
> That familiar things are made new every paragraph will prove. The subject of the poem is an event below the common incidents of common life; nothing real is introduced that is not seen so often as to be no longer regarded, yet the whole detail of a female-day is here brought before us invested with so much art of decoration that, though nothing is disguised, every thing is striking, and we feel all the appetite of curiosity for that from which we have a thousand times turned fastidiously away.[4]

Playing Nestor to the estranged families, and Touchstone to the pedants and poetasters, Pope lights upon a fresh world whose brilliant enchantments are simultaneously imagined into life and searched by the satirist's cooler eye.

[1] Dacier, I. xxiv.
[2] *Iliad* (Preface), I. fol. B2ᵛ.
[3] *Essay on the Writings and Genius of Pope*, 1756, p. 246.
[4] *Lives*, iii. 233–4.

3. Modern Ladies

'Now, Sir, what a pretty Sense these two first Lines makes:

> *Say, what strange Motive, Goddess, cou'd compel*
> *A well-bred Lord t'assault a gentle Belle?*

That is, what could *force* a *well-bred* Man to be damnably rude and to shew himself an errant Clown and a Brute?' [1]

The couplet which so offends the gentleman in Dennis here is one of three which make up the second paragraph of the poem. The other two are:

> Oh say what stranger Cause, yet unexplor'd,
> Cou'd make a gentle *Belle* reject a *Lord*?
> In Tasks so bold, can Little Men engage,
> And in soft Bosoms dwells such mighty Rage?

The penultimate line is thoroughly mock-heroic in its sharp opposition (recalling line 2 of the poem) of the mighty and the trivial; and both the last couplet in particular, and the paragraph in general, recall epic invocations, especially that of the *Aeneid*:

> O Muse! the Causes and the Crimes relate,
> What Goddess was provok'd, and whence her hate:
> For what Offence the Queen of Heav'n began
> To persecute so brave, so just a Man!
> Involv'd his anxious Life in endless Cares,
> Expos'd to Wants, and hurry'd into Wars!
> Can Heav'nly Minds such high resentment show;
> Or exercise their Spight in Human Woe? [2]

But Pope has subtly, under cover of the parody of epic, aroused a new set of tensions in his poem, moving from how heroes ought to behave, in the heroic tradition, to how lords and ladies ought, in deference to good breeding and social restraint. The two kinds of *decorum* are brought into ironic juxtaposition.

The irony is reinforced by setting the language of assault and com-

[1] Dennis, II. 350.   [2] *Aeneid*, i. 11–18.

pulsion, so foreign to the appearance, at least, of the lords and the belles, against the standards of good breeding and politeness. This is done in the form of a joke, it is true—we know 'what Motive' well enough, and it is far from strange—but this opposition of proper behaviour and the impulses which it masks and suppresses reverberates variously right through the poem: in the 'arming' of Belinda, in the elaborate mock-war of the card-game, in Belinda's lament over the betrayal of her 'innocence':

> Oh had I rather un-admir'd remain'd
> In some lone Isle, or distant *Northern* Land;
> Where the gilt *Chariot* never marks the Way,
> Where none learn *Ombre*, none e'er taste *Bohea*! (iv. 153–6)

It is not that the poem always takes the opposition seriously (after all, the loss is of a mere lock of hair), nor that Pope denies social poise its own civilised attractiveness; but that the opposition does frequently result in reducing good breeding to elaborate, hypocritical pretence, and in emphasising the violence and malice all too ready to break through the mask. And with the couplet

> Oh say what stranger Cause, yet unexplor'd,
> Cou'd make a gentle *Belle* reject a *Lord*? (i. 9–10)

we are knee-deep in the morality of the belle's *milieu*, which is dominated by two compulsions—to escape scandalous notoriety and to achieve honourable marriage—both given urgency by the sense of the fragility of both 'honour' and beauty. The belle's position is precarious, her power short-lived. Strange indeed the cause that would prompt her to reject a lover of rank!

Thus, as early as the twelfth line, Pope has firmly and wittily projected into the poem the main tensions on which it will draw. On the one hand, he measures the fops and the belles against the rigorous standards of the heroic code. On the other, he tests the system of elegance and coquetry against the contortions of 'sickly' affectation and the ravages of scandal. Treating the fops as heroes, Pope is exposing the sham in their assumption of dignity. Probing the equilibrium of the belles, he uncovers the strains and perils of their position. Even in the short run, the two activities overlap, each stripping pretences from a society which depends on them. But it has been rightly observed that while we can never believe in the fiction of the fops' heroism, we *can* believe in the fiction of Belinda's divinity,[1] however close it runs to the *clichés* of the *billet-doux*, and for all the bite back in the hyperbole:

> Favours to none, to all she Smiles extends,
> Oft she rejects, but never once offends.
> Bright as the Sun, her Eyes the Gazers strike,
> And, like the Sun, they shine on all alike. (ii. 11–14)

Belinda

Eager to find fault, out of personal animosity, Dennis found Belinda 'a Chimera, not a Character'.[2] His judgment is telling in a way he did not quite intend, just as he reveals more than he knows in his heavily moralistic response to her conduct. Faced with Belinda's outcry after winning the card game, he asks 'is Shouting and Roaring proper for a well-bred lady?', and runs on into a heated denunciation of her (and, by implication, Pope, for not choosing a nicer heroine) as 'an artificial daubing Jilt; a *Tomrig*, a *Virago*, and a *Lady of the Lake*'.[3] Some aspects of Belinda can trouble even a much more sober moralistic reading of the poem. A recent critic, having dwelt on the 'pride' of Belinda at her *toilette*, is disturbed by Pope's praise of her 'graceful Ease, and Sweetness void of Pride' immediately afterwards, and asks 'is [this] inconsistent of Pope?'[4] His answer is that Belinda, as an accomplished coquette, could easily affect composure and humility, and that Pope is actually condemning her for the faults he seems to condone, even approve of.

A better answer, which preserves Pope's moral disapproval without denying Belinda's genuine charm, and the variety in her presentation, lurks behind Dennis's phrase 'a Chimera, not a Character'. Towards the end of 1712, Pope wrote to Caryll mentioning some current worries, and saying:

> As to my writings, I pray God they may never have other enemies than those they have met with—which are, first, priests; secondly, women, who are the fools of priests; and thirdly, beaus and fops, who are the fools of women.[5]

The malleability and changeableness of women remain a source of scorn

[1] See Parkin, p. 112.

[2] Dennis, II. 331.

[3] Dennis, II. 334–5. For the implication of '*Lady of the Lake*' see the poem itself, v. 135–6, and the Twickenham edition, p. 376.

[4] Reichard, p. 895.

[5] Letter of 8 November 1712. *Correspondence*, i. 151.

to Pope. They are, for example, prominent from the start in the Moral
Essay 'Of the Characters of Women': *Epistle to a lady*

> Nothing so true as what you once let fall:
> "Most women have no Characters at all".
> Matter too soft a lasting mark to bear,
> And best distinguish'd by black, brown, or fair.
>   How many Pictures of one Nymph we view,
> All how unlike each other, all how true!
> Arcadia's Countess, here, in ermin'd pride,
> Is there, Pastora by a fountain side.

Belinda is seen in many different lights, not all of them harsh—as
coquette, injured innocent, sweet charmer, society belle, rival of the sun
and murderer of millions. This Cleopatra-like variety indicates simultaneously her charm, a vacuous lack of 'character', the chameleon
coquette's accomplishment as an actress and also the peril of her position,
dangerously 'unfix'd'. At one point the praise of her attractions may be
a mere mask for Pope's satiric attack on the type-figure of the coquette;
at another it is—for all its extravagance—praise no irony can fully under-
mine. The part, or rather parts, which Belinda plays in the elaborate
social drama of manners are at once despicable, laughable, endearing,
precarious, poignant and petty. To shut off some of these aspects of her
is to deplete the poem's rich stock of attitudes—to her as to much else.
For the satire to have much force, we must feel that the belle deserves
serious attention in some measure. By imaginative entry into her world,
we both probe its faults, and sympathise, the better.

The metamorphoses of Belinda are matched by the magical trans-
formations in Pope's presentation of her environment: 'Ovidian graces',
detected by Johnson in the translation of Homer,[1] are here in plenty.
Tortoise and elephant are 'transform'd to *Combs*' of ivory and tortoise-
shell; lacquer tables turn into 'shining Altars of *Japan*'; the mere coffee-
pot is '*China*'s Earth'; and the lost lock of hair becomes, traditionally
enough, a benign new star. Examples are beyond number, and they
commonly exact from the reader a complex response: startlingly re-
creative and enchanting though they are, they mirror the *beau-monde*'s
tendency to deify its trivialities and exalt its social occasions into rites,
while casually neglecting what ought to be sacred:

> Puffs, Powders, Patches, Bibles, Billet-doux. (i. 138)

[1] *Lives*, iii. 239.

C

In a later poem, Lord Timon will exhibit a similar 'disarray of values',[1] his chapel service a light-hearted jig, his dinner a 'solemn sacrifice'.[2]

Belinda herself is associated from the start with hyperbole. She is referred to habitually in terms which suggest inviolate purity, impeccable beauty and even divinity: 'nymph', 'maid', 'the fair', 'virgin', 'goddess', 'Rival of [the sun's] Beams', only rarely by name, and only once as 'a gentle Belle'. Pope was careful to emphasise this distancing process in revising his first text. The phrase 'the Rival of his Beams' replaces the flatly literal description ''midst attending Dames':

> Belinda rose, and 'midst attending Dames
> Launch'd on the bosom of the silver *Thames*. (1712, i. 19–20)

The delighted, amused extravagance of   *(now ii 3–4)*

> *Sol* thro' white Curtains shot a tim'rous Ray,
> And op'd those Eyes that must eclipse the Day (i. 13–14)

was originally far less incautious:

> *Sol* thro' white Curtains did his Beams display,
> And op'd those Eyes which brighter shine than they. (1712, i. 13–14)

Similarly, Pope drops the original description of Belinda as an 'incens'd Virago' (1712, ii. 140), reserving that term for Thalestris (v. 37). He cuts out a reference to 'Dames' (1712, i. 121) and turns the pedestrian 'A Train of well-drest Youths' (1712, i. 21) into 'Fair Nymphs, and well-drest Youths' (ii. 5). He drops altogether the over-specific details of the Baron's propitiatory pyre:

> There lay the Sword-knot *Sylvia*'s Hands had sown,
> With *Flavia*'s Busk that oft had rapp'd his own. (1712, i. 55–6)

There is something conspiratorial in Pope's insistence on the idealising words for Belinda and others; they are, from one point of view, inept exaggerations and weary *clichés*, reflecting the extremes of homage which this society pays to the image of the beautiful woman. But they are also, partly, the traditional language of romantic adulation and compliment, never entirely cheapened, and no more than Belinda's due.

Belinda moves in light as her natural element, and light is diffracted through her whole intensely fragile world. Her petticoat, the vase on the

---

[1] I borrow the phrase from Mack, p. 31.
[2] See Moral Essay IV, 'Of the Use of Riches', 141–68.

dressing-table, the coffee-lamp and coffee-pot are all silver, and her watch chimes with 'a silver Sound'. Her ringlets are 'shining', like the 'Files of Pins', the cards she plays with, Clarissa's scissor-case and the sphere to which the new star, her curls, brings fresh glory. 'Bright' spirits flutter round her, 'Wax-lights in bright Order blaze', the lock is (of course) bright, and she herself is 'bright Nymph' and 'the brightest Fair'. The sun wakes her through white curtains, and white are her robe for the cosmetic ritual, her breast, her ivory neck (*de rigueur*), her combs and the gloves of the beaux. The sylphs are 'glittering', like the youth in Belinda's dream, her jewels, the fatal scissors, and even the dust of broken China vases. She wears 'a sparkling *Cross*'; her cheek turns 'livid' with fright, or 'glows' in slumber; the new star has a 'radiant' trail. Even the Queen of Diamonds achieves the Miltonic look of 'refulgent'.

It is an enchanted, brilliant world, in which, keeping the Cave of Spleen well aside, almost nothing is dull. But the force of all these adjectives of light, both cumulatively and, in many cases, separately, is not simply to convey an impression of shimmering, ideal immaculacy. The poem as a whole, making us aware of much less attractive features of this *milieu*, conditions our response to its brilliance, insinuating its superficiality and transience. Some of the descriptive phrases strike us largely as obligatory gestures, such as 'bright Nymph', 'Silver *Thames*', 'white Breast'. A great many carry ironies either in themselves or pick them up from their immediate contexts. The phrases formed on 'glittering' are a good example of this. 'Glitter' carries, of course, a suggestion of specious superficiality. Belinda's dream-youth has the right attractive *façade*, 'more glitt'ring than a *Birth-night Beau*'. The glitter of the sylphs suggests their fragility, and (metaphorically) the frailty of feminine 'honour' and the changeableness of the coquette. With loss of reputation and virginity Pope associates frail China vessels: once broken, they lie in 'glittring Dust and painted Fragments', and the disparaging force of 'painted' emphasises one aspect of the glitter—'honour' and chastity are, in this society, frail, artificial and easily lost through carelessness. 'Glitt'ring Spoil', an epic periphrasis for captured armour, recalls Dryden's *Aeneid* merely to describe Belinda's jewels: the misapplication is not only a literary joke (and beautifully accurate) but also a reflection of the extravagant seriousness with which the belle-goddess is decked with 'Off'rings'. Lastly, 'glitt'ring *Forfex*', for the scissors, has an epic sound, and achieves both an absurd portentousness and a 'beautiful diminution', moving R. A. Brower to comment:

The essence of Pope's wit in the *Rape of the Lock* lies in this beautiful diminution, where 'beautiful' implies the appeal of the surface and the appeal of a better world of noble manners and actions.[1]

The splendour of Homer lingers vestigially even here.

Creating his brilliant myth of high society in Queen Anne's England, Pope continually prompts us not merely to measure it against the Homeric myths but also to see the element in it of romantic fiction and wishfulness. Beau, belle and witling fail to achieve anything like the heroic attitudes; but repeatedly they strike the obligatory romance postures, and Pope describes them, the better to betray them, with the proper romantic extravagance. He makes the reference to romance quite explicit at one point: when Clarissa gives the Baron the sacrilegious weapon, we get a very literary simile—

> So Ladies in Romance assist their Knight,
> Present the Spear, and arm him for the Fight. (iii. 129–30)

A romance plot is given epic treatment—and after all, romance always took itself very seriously, and to Fielding the terms 'comic romance' and 'comic epic poem in prose' are synonymous.[2] Belinda, dreaming like a romantic heroine, is set against the traditional episodes in which an epic hero is visited by a deity.

In many passages of description and homage Pope strikes a rich vein of ambiguity at the point where epic grandeur and romantic hyperbole overlap. Thalestris 'scatters Deaths around from both her Eyes' (v. 58), the phrase recalling Dryden's Aeneas in battle (*Aeneid*, x. 851): *femme fatale* described to perfection in epic style. The language of combat— 'wounds', 'killing', 'dying', 'perished'—suggests epic warfare but turns out to be the modish euphemisms and sexual innuendos of this world of infatuated make-believe, owing far more to the fair sex's favourite reading, duodecimo novels, than to epic. Addison had made a catalogue of 'metaphorical deaths' in a similar vein:

> wounded by Zelinda's scarlet stocking . . . smitten at the opera by the glance of an eye . . . killed by the tap of a fan on his left shoulder by Coquetilla . . . hurt by the brush of a whalebone petticoat . . . dispatch'd by a smile . . . murder'd by Melissa in her hair.[3]

Pope is enjoying two jokes: revelling in the misapplication of epic terms, he is also taking off the fashionable jargon in which the same misuse is

[1] Brower, p. 144.   [2] See 'Author's Preface' to *Joseph Andrews*.
[3] *Spectator*, no. 377, 13 May 1712.   Quoted by Reichard, pp. 900–1.

already rife. The love-letter's '*Wounds, Charms,* and *Ardors*' are literary fossils. Sir Fopling, dying under Thalestris's murderous glance, clutches at the straw of a current hit-song, and he (and Pope's readers) could no doubt complete the verse:

> These Eyes are made so killing,
> That all who look must dye.
> To Art I'm nothing owing;
> From Art I nothing want:
> These Graces genuine flowing,
> Despise the help of Paint.
> 'Tis Musick but to hear me;
> 'Tis fatal to come near me,
> And Death is in my Eye.[1]

Chloe 'kills' Sir Plume the chivalric, with a mere frown. In the delicious comedy of the sequel he changes identity within a couplet:

> She smil'd to see the doughty Hero slain,
> But at her Smile, the Beau reviv'd again. (v. 69–70)

The Baron himself, awaiting Belinda's terrifying assault, is commended in Dryden's high, heroic style, deflated only by naughty innuendo:

> Nor fear'd the Chief th'unequal Fight to try,
> Who sought no more than on his Foe to die. (v. 77–8)

It would be a pity to take all this too seriously, at the expense of the comedy; but part of the comedy itself derives from Pope's exposure of the element of play-acting and day-dream in the world of intrigue and *billet-doux*. His 'Essay on Homer' makes much the same point: in reading romantic fiction, he argues, 'we but read with a tender Weakness what we can neither apply nor emulate'.[2] Pope may have noted the contrast made by Mme Dacier in much the same vein:

> An *Epic* Poem . . . being the Imitation of an Action, the Poet is oblig'd to represent the Manners exactly the same as they are at the Time he describes them; for, otherwise, his Imitation will be false, and his Heroes will be Romantick Heroes, who have nothing of those they represent but the bare Name, and who neither say, nor act any thing, but what belies their Character, and is contrary to the Customs of those Times, in which they are suppos'd to have liv'd.[3]

[1] From Buononcini's opera *Camilla*. See Twickenham edition, p. 200.
[2] *Iliad*, I. 54.   [3] Dacier, I. xix.

Pope's heroes are, certainly, all too clearly associated with a particular narrow *milieu*, bounded by coffee-house and gilded coach; but they also exist nowhere at all, in the vacuous no-man's-land of posturing fantasy.

And yet, just as there are moments when the epic sonority suits even this poem's dwindled circle of events, so there are times when the romantic hyperboles seem not merely apposite but positively resonant and moving. The closing lines of consolation and compliment to Belinda achieve a fusion of elements from both sources:

> For, after all the Murders of your Eye,
> When, after Millions slain, your self shall die;
> When all those Suns shall sett, as sett they must,
> And all those Tresses shall be laid in Dust;
> *This Lock*, the Muse shall consecrate to Fame,
> And mid'st the Stars inscribe *Belinda*'s Name! (v. 145–50)

Belinda has lost the lock. Luckily, however, the Baron has lost it too, and is therefore powerless to rob her of a possession yet more precious. Had he been able to vaunt the curl to a succession of envying, prurient fops, her reputation—worth more than ringlets, more than 'Ease, Pleasure, Virtue, All' (iv. 106)—would be destroyed. To lose such a trophy is, for Belinda, to suffer notoriety as a 'degraded Toast'. Given her code of behaviour, that is the worst imaginable fate.

Reading the poem, we disapprove of the scale of values that takes minor incidents so seriously. But we also feel our way, as Pope does, into a sympathetic appreciation of *why*, given that scale, the loss of the lock is really calamitous. Into this aspect of Belinda's predicament, the sylphs are an invaluable guide.

The Sylphs

When Clarissa, with 'tempting Grace', has given the Baron the scissors, only the insubstantial sylphs stand between him and the possession of this latest and best trophy in his rake's progress. The condition of their defence of the lock, indeed of their guarding Belinda at all, is clear: she must reject all earthly lovers, remaining (as Ariel puts it) 'innocent' and 'chaste'. Her downfall is sped by her allowing herself to entertain thoughts of a lover: the slip costs her the lock and very nearly her 'honour'.

In the sylphs we witness a delightful down-scaling of the epic Machines, light by any heroic standards and assailed by unholy panic at moments of crisis, yet adapted in every detail, physical and metaphysical, to their rôle as Belinda's intimates and counsellors. They reflect the beauty and explain the perilous tangles of conventions and anxieties that make up Belinda's day. In considering them, we sense at once the tremulous intensity, the sensuous richness, with which Belinda is surrounded, and the pressures and apprehensions to which she is subjected, in part unknowingly. Her beauty is, like their colours, ephemeral; her moment of uncommitted conquest as fragile as they; and they are as caught up as she in the intricate social structure which excites her dreams of power and is baited like a snare. As in Homer, where 'heav'nly Breasts with human Passions rage' (v. 46), so in Pope the celestials mingle with their transcendence more than a wisp of human puzzlement, vanity and pride.

Pope's observation of the *mores* of Queen Anne Society, for which the sylphs are both mirror and mock-apotheosis, made its own discoveries along lines already familiar to theatre-goers and the readers of Addison, Steele and others. The Restoration dramatists, and the essayists in their wake, had familiarized certain type-figures in this brilliant, merciless setting. Again and again, Pope takes hints from these sources, or at least echoes them so closely that they afford a welcome aid to interpretation.[1] The danger is that in discussing what Belinda is 'really' up to—whether she is a 'bride-to-be' or a 'coquette *par excellence*'[2]—we will anatomise her out of existence, turning a satirical comedy of manners into a too severe and single-minded *exemplum* on the errors of her ways.

Belinda, in the moments before waking—when she forgets the whole vision in a trice—dreams that the most winning of beaux tells her how the sylphs guide and protect her in the intricate vocation of combining endless provocation with inviolate maidenhood. The unsuspected implications and false logic of his account, reflecting the predicament of the 'tender Maid' in a circle of rakes, reduce his armoury of noble terms such as 'innocent', 'honour' and 'purity' to the level of muddle and sham. Himself a metamorphosed coquette in disguise (!), citing the very best Miltonic precedent—

> For Spirits, freed from mortal Laws, with ease
> Assume what Sexes and what Shapes they please (i. 69–70)—

[1] The relevant essays are noted by Reichard and, of course, the Twickenham edition. For the plays, see M. Goldstein, *Pope and the Augustan Stage*, 1958.

[2] See Reichard, p. 889.

he understands all too easily the way into a belle's heart. He assures
Belinda promptly of her own importance, then of the immortality of her
feminine delight in the civilised trappings which she might think
transient (and we think trivial):

> Think not, when Woman's transient Breath is fled,
> That all her Vanities at once are dead:
> Succeeding Vanities she still regards,
> And tho' she plays no more, o'erlooks the Cards.
> Her Joy in gilded Chariots, when alive,
> And Love of *Ombre*, after Death survive. (i. 51–6)

His voice glides smoothly in Belinda's ear, untroubled by the words
which carry, for us, destructive implications ('Vanities' and 'gilded'), or
by the hollow echo of a couplet in Dryden's *Aeneid* describing the sur-
vival of nobler emotions in the after-life of heroes:

> The love of Horses which they had, alive,
> And care of Chariots, after Death survive. (*Aeneid*, vi. 890)

He is there, he whispers, to guard her 'purity' according to sylphic
theology:

> Whoever fair and chaste
> Rejects Mankind, is by some *Sylph* embrac'd. (i. 67–8)

Celestially defended, the 'melting Maids' are safe, for what we call
'Honour' is really no more than Providence:

> 'Tis but their *Sylph*, the wise Celestials know,
> Tho' *Honour* is the Word with Men below. (i. 77–8)

Reassuring Belinda in this way, Ariel is in effect undermining her moral
position, taking away with one hand the credit he gives with the other,
and all unknowingly. He explains glibly how her defence is achieved.
A maid would fall to Florio if Damon weren't, distractingly, at hand, if
'old Impertinence' were not expelled 'by new', and if the sylphs did not
pander to the insatiable appetite for *trivia* and trinkets:

> With varying Vanities, from ev'ry Part,
> They shift the moving Toyshop of their Heart. (i. 99–100)

What we call 'levity' in women, says Ariel, is the effect of the same
divine guidance as determined their 'honour': the concealed implication,
that the two qualities are roughly on a par, almost the same thing, is
devastating. But Ariel runs blithely on, to warn Belinda in epic style of

the foreshadowed 'dread Event', ending with a plea for caution from the lips that have just encouraged flirtatiousness:

> Beware of all, but most beware of Man! (i. 114)

In a trice, as if to follow the surreptitious, not the overt, logic of his speech, Belinda forgets it all. The vision had, after all, made her blush; now she succumbs to the 'new Impertinence' of the love-letter's mannered protestations. The sylphs aid her at the ritual of self-adoration in the dressing-mirror, and she sails up river, faithful for the moment to the very letter of Ariel's conditions for undertaking to protect her:

> Favours to none, to all she Smiles extends;
> Oft she rejects, but never once offends. (ii. 11–12)

Ariel's list of possible calamities, in his speech during the voyage, is celebrated as an unknowing exposure of the belle's jumbled notions of comparative value:

> Whether the Nymph shall break *Diana*'s Law,
> Or some frail *China* Jar receive a Flaw,
> Or stain her Honour, or her new Brocade,
> Forget her Pray'rs, or miss a Masquerade,
> Or lose her Heart, or Necklace, at a Ball;
> Or whether Heav'n has doom'd that *Shock* must fall. (ii. 105–10)

The paired calamities are not merely ludicrously ill-assorted contrasts. There is a metaphorical transference across the gap, so that one item in a pair can almost become a symbol for the other. The properties of china suggest how easily chastity might be lost in the world of philanderers, and how irreparably. 'Honour', to the belle, is a publicly worn accessory, like her brocade—easily stained, but if the stain weren't seen it would not matter. She would take a masquerade with 'religious' seriousness, and her prayers with a masquerade's flippancy. And her heart can be lost as easily—again and again—as a necklace, which is no less precious.

The confusion of values is not, of course, a waywardness of the sylphs, but a disorder of the whole social system. One critic has pointed out: 'As far as the fashionable world is concerned, big things, like the loss of virtue, may have no important consequences; whereas little things, the snipping of a curl, may be disastrous.'[1] Not only mock-heroically, nor only in the romantic hyperboles, in the belle's self-conceit or the panic of the sylphs, is the lock important. Given the belle's precarious position,

[1] Parkin, p. 114.

the smallest chink in her armour, the loss of the merest token, and all her 'honour' *is* 'in a Whisper lost' (iv. 110). And yet, if she risks nothing, she can fear the fate of those other familiar figures of the essayists—the 'scornful Virgins who their Charms survive' (iv. 4), learning in em-bittered middle age to respect too late Clarissa's daunting proverb, 'she who scorns a Man, must die a Maid' (v. 28).

And the sylphs know too, in their delicate way, that the plain facts behind the courtly conventions and elaborate skirmishing are sexual. The petticoat, which attracts but conceals, is the belle's vital shield:

> Oft have we known that sev'nfold Fence to fail,
> Tho' stiff with Hoops, and arm'd with Ribs of Whale.
> Form a strong Line about the Silver Bound,
> And guard the wide Circumference around. (ii. 119–22)

Clarissa   Clarissa's speech important

The Moral Essay 'Of the Characters of Women', which begins by regretting feminine lack of 'character', is brought to a close on a com-plimentary address to Martha Blount:

> The gen'rous God, who Wit and Gold refines,
> And ripens Spirits as he ripens Mines,
> Kept Dross for Duchesses, the world shall know it,
> To you gave Sense, Good-humour, and a Poet. (289–92)

Either Martha or her sister Teresa was the 'Miss Blount' to whom Pope addressed his epistle 'With the Works of Voiture', which was completed some two years before *The Rape of the Lock*. One paragraph in particular invites comparison with Clarissa's speech:

> But, Madam, if the Fates withstand, and you
> Are destin'd *Hymen*'s willing Victim too,
> Trust not too much your now resistless Charms,
> Those, Age or Sickness, soon or late, disarms;
> *Good humour* only teaches Charms to last,
> Still makes new Conquests, and maintains the past:
> Love, rais'd on Beauty, will like That decay,
> Our Hearts may bear its slender Chain a Day,
> As flow'ry Bands in Wantonness are worn;
> A Morning's Pleasure, and at Evening torn;
> *This* binds in Ties more easie, yet more strong,
> The willing Heart, and only holds it long. (57–68)

Although Clarissa's speech was not added to *The Rape* until 1717, Pope no
doubt still recalled the terms of this paragraph, as he did when writing the
poem's Dedication, appealing to feminine good sense and good humour.
The flattering 'glories' of social esteem and privilege are, Clarissa
argues, achieved in vain

> Unless good Sense preserve what Beauty gains. (v. 16)

Old age and small-pox will make their inroads, beauty will decay, for all
the gaiety of dancing, and for all the time lavished on dress. There is
nothing for it but for women to make good use of their power, and
'keep good Humour still whate'er we lose' (v. 30). Her conclusion is
(ostensibly, at any rate) impeccable:

> And trust me, Dear! good Humour can prevail,
> When Airs, and Flights, and Screams, and Scolding fail.
> Beauties in vain their pretty Eyes may roll;
> Charms strike the Sight, but Merit wins the Soul. (v. 31–4)

The virtue Clarissa inculcates and Pope himself, early and late in his
career, set much store by, is 'a real virtue, but a "smiling" one, and
attainable within the limits of a worldly society more inclined to trust
intelligence than enthusiasm'.[1]

Those limits are precisely and repeatedly emphasised in the course of
the speech. In part they indicate Clarissa's clear grasp of the contin-
gencies and the pleasures which make difficult the retention of a consistent moral attitude in her particular sphere of interest. In part they
indicate limitations in her range of vision. Seeing through the vanity of
the belle's domain, she has choric status in the poem, at the cost of
Thalestris' worldly, hysterical concern for reputation, and the sylphs'
unabashed love of the 'varying Vanities' of high society life. In so far as
her argument is based on a sober recognition of the mutability of charm,
beauty and life itself, it carries an 'absolute' quality which the echoes of
Sarpedon's great address to Glaucus, its masculine counterpart, buttress
rather than devalue:

> But since, alas! ignoble Age must come,
> Disease, and Death's inexorable Doom;
> The Life, which others pay, let us bestow,
> And give to Fame what we to Nature owe;
> Brave tho' we fall, and honour'd if we live,
> Or let us Glory gain, or Glory give! (*Iliad*, xii. 391–6)

[1] Brower, p. 160.

But there is, of course, another side to the picture. Pope chose to give the speech to the very person who had presented the Baron with the 'fatal Sheers'. He dextrously suggests a rather *blasé*, worldly tone of address, making the speech dramatically vivid, but also tying the 'moral' down to *a* speaker in *a* context. Clarissa is cosy, feminine, reassuring: 'To patch, nay ogle', 'Nor could it sure be such a Sin', 'And trust me, Dear!'

Nor is she always by any means so absolute or disinterested as she might seem. She evidently prizes the 'glories' (a telling overstatement) of the theatre box and the coach besieged by flattering dandies, and we may remember how the sylphs, in the card game, relish the way in which guardianship of the higher cards indicates higher celestial rank:

> For *Sylphs*, yet mindful of their ancient Race,
> Are, as when Women, wondrous fond of Place. (iii. 35–6)

Her argument is furtively, delicately placed and measured even while she develops it. There are telling declensions from the heroic parallels: from

> Why on these Shores are we with Joy survey'd,
> Admir'd as Heroes, and as Gods obey'd? (*Iliad*, xii. 377–8)

to

> Why deck'd with all that Land and Sea afford,
> Why Angels call'd, and Angel-like ador'd? (v. 11–12)

(recalling Belinda at the dressing-table, and intercepted short of a positive claim by 'call'd' and '-like'); or from

> 'Tis ours, the Dignity they give, to grace;
> The first in Valour, as the first in Place; (*Iliad*, xii. 381–2)

to

> That Men may say, when we the Front-box grace,
> Behold the first in Virtue, as in Face! (v. 17–18)

(recalling, with a difference, Thalestris' concern for what *They* say, and with a possible pun on 'face' as both beauty and boldness of countenance).

Several couplets in her speech subtly qualify her concern for the changeless aspects of the human condition, and restrict her reaching towards an absolute attitude, by presenting a much less disinterested train of thought. For instance, the reflection

> How vain are all these Glories, all our Pains,

is immediately followed and in part diluted by

> Unless good Sense preserve what Beauty gains. (v. 15–16)

A more glaring example occurs in the couplet

> Since painted, or not painted, all shall fade,
> And she who scorns a Man, must die a Maid. (v. 27–8)

Here the grave recognition of transience slides casually into an aphoristic endorsement of opportunism in the battle of the sexes. This in turn carries over into the recommendation 'well our Pow'r to use', from which she climbs again to a position of mature, sensible resignation:

> And keep good Humour still whate'er we lose. (v. 30)

Clarissa's speech undoubtedly carries the 'moral' of the poem, touching some of its deepest chords, while at the same time exhibiting the radical limitations of even this degree of maturity in the society in which it is so firmly set. She is in earnest, but well this side of asceticism. To say, on the one hand, that she is 'only seemingly concerned with the impeccable moral that feminine charms strike the sight but merit . . . wins the soul',[1] or, on the other hand, that she is simply Pope's mouthpiece,[2] is to fail to respond fully to the speech's complexity in its context. The two statements are not contradictory; they need making simultaneously.

Thalestris

To the 'fierce Virago' of the poem, Clarissa's moralising smacks of prudery (v. 36). Her own incendiary speech in the preceding canto, however, stood on its moral dignity:

> Gods! shall the Ravisher display your Hair,
> While the Fops envy, and the Ladies stare!
> *Honour* forbid! at whose unrival'd Shrine
> Ease, Pleasure, Virtue, All, our Sex resign. (iv. 103–6)

For 'Honour' she would sacrifice 'Virtue' along with *everything else*: the catalogue in the last of these lines rises with carefree lack of logic to a rhetorical peak in the grand word 'All'. It is a devastating climax. As a collective for the first three items in her list, 'All' exposes the hollowness

[1] Parkin, p. 171.
[2] See Cleanth Brooks, *The Well-Wrought Urn*, London, 1949, pp. 88–9.

and muddle of her values; as a euphemism for virginity, it insinuates that reputation is worth more than chastity.[1] Thalestris is demonstrating in advance the 'Airs, and Flights, and Screams, and Scolding' which Clarissa will take to task. Were Belinda to fall victim to malicious gossip, Thalestris would be unlikely to stand by her—to do so would be 'Infamy'. Sooner than let that happen, she exclaims, change the whole microcosm of leisure and privilege, disrupt the elements, and abandon the whole range of ladies' pets:

> Men, Monkeys, Lap-dogs, Parrots, perish all! (iv.120)

But a deeper note is also struck, as so often in this poem, in a context of shallowness and muddle. Within two couplets, the speech catches an adroitly ill-assorted sequence of tones, from 'epic' (Hecuba forseeing Hector's death), through 'contemporary' (with a cheapness that contrives to be touching), to a sonorous close:

> Methinks already I your Tears survey,
> Already hear the horrid things they say,
> Already see you a degraded Toast,
> And all your Honour in a Whisper lost! (iv. 107-10)

4. Heroi-Comical

Rituals

> How but in custom and in ceremony
> Are innocence and beauty born?
> W. B. Yeats, *A Prayer for my Daughter*

Ariel concludes his warning to Belinda with the high Virgilian plea 'oh Pious Maid beware!' Within moments she is engaged in the secular pieties of self-adoration at her mirror. The prominence in Virgil's epic of rituals of propitiation and commemoration throws attention upon 'pius Aeneas', and emphasises the awareness of the higher dispensation in whose light (and shadow) the human beings conduct their affairs.

[1] This is, of course, the clear implication of Belinda's rash couplet at the end of this canto (iv. 175–6). Only *just* delicate enough to give to Belinda, the couplet was originally spoken, with a slight difference, by Thalestris (1712, ii. 19–20). The transfer was made in 1714. See also p. 58 below.

Belinda's world, in its turn, is preoccupied with ceremonies. These are sometimes beautiful, sometimes absurd, never innocent: Belinda's *toilette*, the Baron's amatory pyre, the serving of coffee. In the contrast with epic, the triviality and narcissism of such rituals is manifest. They are enacted in a moral vacuum. Each of them, furthermore, is a significant stage in the elaborate battle of wits and eyes which culminates in the actual 'rape'. At the dressing-table Belinda prepares for conquest; by the pyre the Baron prays for, and over the coffee-table plots for, possession of the trophy which is to top his fake renown. The absurd earnestness of these preparations is very aptly exposed in the emphasis on ritual: it suggests not only misapplied seriousness, but also 'going through the motions', a comedy of obligatory postures.

The 'toilet's greasy task', as Pope in another mood could call it,[1] is here subjected to a scrutiny no less harsh in its implications, but masking them with a fastidiousness nicely suited to this context—beauty putting on its required face. Commentaries on the scene have dwelt on the disparagement which Pope's description carries, and rightly, but at the risk of obscuring the element of genuine amused acquiescence, even enchantment, in Pope's attitude. While the hyperbole of the passage largely exposes the inflated, culpably vain seriousness Belinda brings to her self-worship, it is also the vehicle of a delighted play of imagination and wit over the beautiful intense trivialities of this *milieu*:

> This Casket *India*'s glowing Gems unlocks,
> And all *Arabia* breathes from yonder Box. (i. 133–4)

To the *Spectator*'s drily confidential anatomies of contemporary manners, which repeatedly catch belles and beaux in similar infatuated postures, Pope brings a sense of elegance and sensuous fullness which can in some respects withstand and survive the ironic implications. His hyperboles, conspiring against Belinda by mimicking her vanity, retain a note of sincere homage.

Assured only moments earlier of the care which the 'wise Celestials' exercise over her, Belinda in the glass discovers her own sufficient divinity. The eyes that are to 'eclipse the Day' are infatuated with her self-created 'heav'nly Image', like Milton's Eve at her creation, delighted with her 'smooth watry image' in the lake.[2] The passage consistently projects a series of ideal images of Belinda, matching her own idolatry:

[1] Moral Essay II, 25.
[2] *Paradise Lost*, iv. 449 ff. Cited by Reichard, p. 895.

'Nymph intent', 'the Goddess', and 'awful Beauty' arming for her moments of total (and indiscriminate) conquest.[1] Pope maintains a double suggestion, first, that she is merely accentuating her natural beauty—'awakening' her grace, 'calling forth' her face's wonders—and second, that she is engaged in jobbery and deception—'repairing' her smiles, purifying the glow of her cheeks in an uncomfortably close echo of the 'young *Coquettes*' who, in Ariel's words, can produce at will 'a bidden Blush'. Belinda is no more ingenuous than they.

The whole world does homage with its 'Off'rings', and at Belinda's side her priestess works, until the anticlimactic moment which grounds the whole passage, finally, in the merely domestic and mundane:

> And *Betty*'s praised for Labours not her own.

The mock-heroic element in this scene is present in the meticulous adjustment of the arming of the epic hero to this more feminine world, where the niceties of description have their own different justification, whether or not satirically weighted. Belinda arms for a battle she cannot take less than seriously, dressing to kill: the epic phrase for armour, 'glitt'ring Spoil', wittily suggests this, and also fits to a nicety the ransacking of the globe which feminine beauty takes, quite nonchalantly, as its due.

Her adversary, romantically awake before dawn (unlike the more usual 'sleepless Lovers' who stir at noon), is in no less 'pious' mood. He lights his pyre of tokens in a ludicrous, no-man's-land between epic conflict—

> Resolv'd to win, he meditates the way,
> By Force to ravish, or by Fraud betray (ii. 31–2)—

and romance histrionics—

> With tender *Billet-doux* he lights the Pyre,
> And breathes three am'rous Sighs to raise the Fire. (ii. 41–2)

He, too, has deities to worship ('chiefly *Love*'), and Pope introduces his rites with a sonorous six lines, dense with impressive allusions and culminating in a couplet in which an epic formula ('fraud or force') is insinuated into a neat *exposé* of the token-hunter's lack of scruple:

> For when Success a Lover's Toil attends,
> Few ask, if Fraud or Force attain'd his Ends. (ii. 33–4)

[1] The indiscriminateness is emphasised in ii. 13–14.

In the Baron's plots, no less than at Belinda's mirror, all is fair in love or war, and love is a campaign. Tenderly, he ignites 'all the Trophies' of his salacious career, on a modish altar which matches Belinda's 'Bibles, Billet-doux'. The 'Pow'rs' respond to his prayer with an ambiguous answer that echoes, by way of Dryden, all the way to Olympus:

> Apollo heard, and granting half his Pray'r,
> Shuffled in Winds the rest, and toss'd in empty Air.
>
> *(Aeneid, xi. 1165)*

The comic disproportion mirrors the seriousness with which the Baron views his philandering pranks. In that violently distorting glass he is, paradoxically, reduced to his proper size.

The ceremony of taking coffee 'religiously' is framed by ominous epic *sententiae*, dwelling on man's blindness to consequence and on his sinister inventiveness in the cause of evil. The immaculate ritual, indispensable to the politicians—men of such virtuosity in combining amorous manoeuvres with more public diplomacy (iii. 5–6)—is the back-cloth for the Baron's furtive scheming. This insinuates once again that appearances in this *milieu* can mask deception and intrigue only too easily: but the insinuation is lightly managed. By a wicked pun on 'Vapours' (coffee-fumes and melancholy), Pope deflates modish hypochondria and the satanic Baron at a single blow.

The epic feasts, Pope was to argue later, are not uncouth, but an example of primitive heroic simplicity, honest epic gorging. The coffee ritual is complicated, diminutive, precarious. It is a moment of high sophistication and poise, qualities brought out by the presence of the sylphs, with their magical absurdity:

> Some o'er her Lap their careful Plumes display'd,
> Trembling, and conscious of the rich Brocade. (iii. 115–16)

Intimately, they enact Belinda's own preoccupations.

Spleen

The belle's poise is built upon, and in its turn threatened by, personal and social tensions. The winning ease of Belinda on the barge is far from artless; slander and profligacy are on the alert to exploit her merest stumble; her beauty is, in the nature of things, ephemeral; and the twin penalties of any error in steering the tricky course between the excitement of men's interest and the refusal of male advances are equally daunting—notoriety and bitter, virginal age.

D

In the comic climaxes of the poem—the women's outcries, Belinda's shouts, the battle for the lock—suppressed energies break through the civilised veneer. In the Cave of Spleen, Pope probes the waste land on the margins of the *beau monde's* brightly lit, seemingly secure territory. The inhabitants of this underworld, from the Goddess of Spleen to Ill-Nature and the melancholic phantoms, are only partly the caricatures of a fashionable malady's treasured symptoms and bored prerogatives. They are also the 'Parts of Nature' hidden beneath the 'Robe of Quality',[1] the sinister counterparts of much that the poem tends to take quite lightly, or appears to:

> The Fair-ones feel such Maladies as these,
> When each new Night-Dress gives a new Disease. (iv. 37–8)

The second Moral Essay dissects closely comparable figures. For Affectation, it anatomises the plight of the lady who

> in sweet vicissitude appears
> Of Mirth and Opium, Ratafie and Tears, (109–10)

and for Ill-Nature, the 'ancient Maid', it offers a series of aging puppets whom society has relegated to the contortions of impotent disappointment:

> As Hags hold Sabbaths, less for joy than spight,
> So these their merry, miserable Night;
> Still round and round the Ghosts of Beauty glide,
> And haunt the places where their Honour dy'd. (239–42)

The Cave of Spleen is full of similar shadows, darker cousins of the sylphs.

The hallucinatory effects of 'the Vapours' in the Cave are largely derived, directly or indirectly, from Burton's *Anatomy of Melancholy*. Pope's catalogue begins—as Warburton points out—by treating as melancholic illusions what Pope was to call 'the dreams of splenetic enthusiasts and solitaries, who fall in love with saints':

> Dreadful, as Hermit's Dreams in haunted Shades,
> Or bright as Visions of expiring Maids. (iv. 41–2)

Then the scenic effects of contemporary opera and pantomime are presented as caused by spleen—stunts, as it were, like the hallucinations.

---

[1] Moral Essay II, 187–90.

But the astounding list of 'Bodies chang'd to various Forms by *Spleen*' deriving from Burton, brings the whole fantasy home to roost:

> Here living *Teapots* stand, one Arm held out,
> One bent; the Handle this, and that the Spout:
> A Pipkin there like *Homer's Tripod* walks;
> Here sighs a Jar, and there a Goose-pye talks;
> Men prove with Child, as pow'rful Fancy works,
> And Maids turn'd Bottels, call aloud for Corks. (iv. 49–54)

Burton had dealt, more bashfully, with symptoms of 'Maids', Nuns', and Widows' Melancholy'. The cure for such feminine vapours, he had suggested, 'is to see them well placed, and married to good husbands in due time'.[1] The Cave of Spleen is partly a limbo of sexual and social frustrations, as clearly in the sighing jar and the shouting bottles as in the allegorical figures of Ill-Nature and Affectation. Umbriel, addressing the Goddess, boasts of his prowess in suggestive practical jokes: spoiling graces, raising pimples, changing complexions of losers at cards, rumpling petticoats and making cuckolds. He is rewarded with a whole armoury of feminine intensities, and goes back to give suppressed frustrations their hysterical outlet:

> There she collects the Force of Female Lungs,
> Sighs, Sobs, and Passions, and the War of Tongues.
> A Vial next she fills with fainting Fears,
> Soft Sorrows, melting Griefs, and flowing Tears. (iv. 83–6)

The whole episode of the Cave is partly a hilarious romp among well-to-do hyponchondriacs, the devotees of 'sweet vicissitude', and partly a nightmare tour through the landscape of *ennui*, repression and distorted impulse which lies so close to the scene of Belinda's perilous gaiety. These are the bogeys behind Thalestris' fear of scandal and its aftermath, and behind Clarissa's warning to the maid who scorns a man.

At several other moments in the poem the more sinister aspect of the Cave finds parallels. In each case the parallel passage is a satiric catalogue —and this is significant: no other device conveys so decisively the muddle, the breakdown of vital distinctions, the corruption of sanctions, which are the most alarming features of this casual but intense society. At the opening of canto III, such a list brackets together, with revealing nonchalance, the domestic scenes of the merchant returning home and

[1] *Anatomy of Melancholy*, Everyman edition, vol. I, p. 417.

the belle at her mirror, with the off-hand inequities they care little about. The juxtaposition throws oblique light on a whole rotten social structure of corrupt and vacuous privilege. The first paragraph of canto IV, similarly, performs a rhetorical *tour de force*, in which epic passions alternate with social frets and disappointments:

> Not youthful Kings in Battel seiz'd alive,
> Not scornful Virgins who their Charms survive,
> Not ardent Lovers robb'd of all their Bliss,
> Not ancient Ladies when refus'd a Kiss,
> Not Tyrants fierce that unrepenting die,
> Not *Cynthia* when her *Manteau's* pinn'd awry . . . (iv. 3–8)

Finally, there is the catalogue of 'things lost on Earth', which have their own limbo. They range from collectors' *trivia* to the hearts of lovers, from broken vows to the deceptions of self-interest and the desperate shifts of pain:

> The Courtier's Promises, and Sick Man's Pray'rs,
> The Smiles of Harlots, and the Tears of Heirs. (v. 119–20)

Pope in such catalogues lets us see with what blindness and with what hypocrisy the *beau monde* keeps up the costly fiction of the bland exterior.

The Battles

Belinda herself changes complexions at a losing game, as Umbriel would put it, during the battle of cards on the 'Velvet Plain'. She wins it, only to have to fight again in the tussle for possession of the lock of hair. Both battles are given ironically inflated treatment, catching repeated echoes of Troy and Carthage in the civilised corridors of Hampton Court. A literary joke, this is also a disparaging reflection on current misconceptions of relative importance, and on Belinda's inability to take the assorted misfortunes of 'Ruin, and *Codille*' with Martha Blount's mature dispassion:

> Lets Fops or Fortune fly which way they will;
> Disdains all loss of Tickets, or Codille;
> Spleen, Vapours, or Small-pox, above them all,
> And Mistress of herself, tho' China fall.[1]

[1] Moral Essay II, 265–8.

The card-battle is heralded in terms which carry an ambiguity important for the consideration of both conflicts:

> *Belinda* now, whom Thirst of Fame invites,
> Burns to encounter two adventrous Knights,
> At *Ombre* singly to decide their Doom;
> And swells her Breast with Conquests yet to come. (iii. 25–8)

Beneath the absurd hyperbole of these lines, the suggestion is strong that the card-game, like the 'games' of 'singing, laughing, ogling, *and all that*', is a vicarious amorous skirmish. 'The Virgin' is exposed to 'wily Arts' which threaten to rob her of the initiative, but which she outmanoeuvres to maintain the uncommitted position, 'fair and chaste', which Ariel recommends for the coquette. Faced with 'Ruin, and *Codille*', Belinda's panic is very like Cynthia's pampered anger over her ill-arranged *manteau*—the wood has been lost for the trees. But within the dramatic context, there is a sense in which the stakes *are* high: one word kills a reputation, and the vultures are at hand to interpret 'Motions, Looks, and Eyes'. On the phrase 'Ruin, and *Codille*', it has been said: 'If at one level the disparity tickles the catastrophe with bathos, at another level it insinuates that the beaten player would be a fallen woman.' [1] Belinda feels she must yield nothing to the Baron, in earnest or in jest. It is vital not to take the insinuation too seriously; but without it, the mock-heroic joke becomes a mere exercise, though a very efficient one, in overblown description.

Belinda's generalship begins with *panache*, outdoing her epic predecessors in the divine loftiness of her opening words:

> *Let Spades be Trumps!* she said, and Trumps they were. (iii. 46)

Her early moves are sweepingly successful, and reach a climax when she overcomes 'mighty *Pam*', Knave of Clubs and Sarpedon of this less gory field. But Fate swings the initiative to the Baron, who causes epic havoc with his Diamonds and 'wins (oh shameful Chance!) the *Queen of Hearts*'. All depends on the last trick, and Belinda wins because she holds, appropriately, the highest card of the suit the Baron leads—Hearts.

Her triumph is short-lived. The 'honours' of the card-game are succeeded by the Baron's epic vaunt, waving aloft the lock of hair, 'The long-contended Honours of her Head' (iv. 140). The key-term 'honours' recalls Dryden's *Aeneid*, and is found in Pope's *Iliad* too,

[1] Reichard, p. 897.

associated with sacredness and ritual. The epic contrast with Belinda's and the Baron's hollow boasts is sharp, especially in close proximity with the word 'Honour', which has suffered a parallel decline (iv. 105–6).

The second battle is a preposterous sequence of antics, which Pope not once takes seriously. It is the farcical counterpart of the romantic hyperboles with which the poem has associated Belinda, and women in general: lines like

> Now awful Beauty puts on all its Arms (i. 139)

and

> This Nymph, to the Destruction of Mankind,
> Nourish'd two Locks (ii. 19–20)

topple over into full absurdity in the erotic slaughter of the fops. Pope admired, in Homer's accounts of battles, 'that *Diversity* in the *Deaths* of his *Warriors*, which he has supply'd with the vastest Fertility of Invention that ever was', and remarked upon 'the several *Postures* in which his Heroes are represented either fighting or falling' and 'the Difference of the *Wounds* that are given'.[1] Pope delightedly offers the 'polite' version of these Homeric climaxes, scaled down as neatly as Ariel's list of heroic punishments (ii. 123–36). The beaux achieve appropriate perorations in which amorous complaint and high epic gesture are confounded:

> O *cruel Nymph! a living Death I bear*,
> Cry'd *Dapperwit*, and sunk beside his Chair. (v. 61–2)

The wit in such lines makes the introductory literary reference to epic ('So when bold *Homer* . . .') look crude, especially as that reference has the ill-luck to follow a brilliantly funny couplet which describes the human tussle with simultaneous epic grandeur and literal truth:

> No common Weapons in their Hands are found,
> Like Gods they fight, nor dread a mortal Wound. (v. 43–4) [2]

Jove surveys the battle, and below him Pope's Machines await their chance to emulate the Homeric gods and intervene.

[1] *Iliad*, II. 322.

[2] 'nor dread a mortal Wound' can be read as either 'women's weapons can't kill' or 'the combatants, fearless as the Gods, would hardly want to avoid a fatal (amorous) wound: women's weapons are, deliciously, murderous'. The absurd diminutive is at iii. 152, describing the sylphs: 'Airy Substance soon unites again'.

Heroes

> Had some brave Chief this martial Scene beheld,
> By *Pallas* guarded thro' the dreadful Field,
> Might Darts be bid to turn their Points away,
> And Swords around him innocently play,
> The War's whole Art with Wonder had he seen,
> And counted Heroes where he counted Men.
>
> > (*Iliad*, iv. 631–6)

Less than heroes, Pope's beaux are also less than men; but they are certainly practised in the 'whole Art' of their intricate warfare. It is, by convention as by hyperbole, an 'unequal Fight' (v. 77)—the men worshipping and pleading for favours, the ladies dispensing mortal wounds and withholding their cure. In

> She smil'd to see the doughty Hero slain,
> But at her Smile, the Beau reviv'd again. (v. 69–70)

the ineptness of beauty's willing victims attains a comic pathos.

Of course, the poem affects a fully credulous approval of the courtly *status quo*, woman's invincibility and man's subservience, the better to subject it to ironic inspection. Its technical ease and delicacy mirror the feminine qualities, the better to mask a satiric robustness and capacity to shock—the trick used by the wolf in Little Red Riding Hood. The women, and the aura through which they are to be worshipped, are its main focus of interest—inviting, but in part immune from, Pope's satiric eye. The men, by comparison, are skittles easily knocked down. Women dominate them in the poem as easily as in the sex-war. Unless by 'force or fraud', men cannot win.

The Baron plots and prays for a minor makeshift victory, which will gain him credit as a lady-killer with the salacious. He is, in their eyes as in his own, 'adventurous'—the mock-heroic description is *dramatically* accurate. At the moment of the rape, he breaks into high rhetoric, catching echoes of the speech in which Aeneas, pleading with Dido to let the Trojans stay in Carthage, vows

> While rowling Rivers into Seas shall run,
> And round the space of Heav'n the radiant Sun;
> While Trees the Mountain tops with Shades supply,
> Your Honour, Name, and Praise shall never dye.[1]

[1] *Aeneid*, i. 854–7.

The Baron's flourish is, of course, *self*-congratulatory. Apart from the irony of the philanderer's celebrating his own 'Honour' (the *beau monde* is basically narcissistic), his rhetorical catalogue slides unconcernedly from grand gesture to

> As long as *Atalantis* shall be read,
> Or the small Pillow grace a Lady's Bed . . . (iii. 165–6)

All's one to the Baron, but romances and assignations are his element, and '*Snuff-boxes* and *Tweezer-Cases*' adequate containers for his wits.

Astonishingly, Pope caps the Baron's absurdity with a grandiose peroration to the third canto, in which such catastrophes as the fall of Troy are linked with the loss of the curls. But this time the bathos is not merely hollow extravagance: reinforcing the theme of transience, it makes the lock of hair lamentably puny, alarmingly vulnerable, while putting its loss into a belittling perspective. When we last leave the Baron, in the last canto, he is defeated in the very moment of his finest escapade, Belinda's vanquished adorer, a slave in love's 'Labyrinths'. The bluff of the metaphorical death has been called, by Belinda's bodkin.

Lapdogs, parrots, china vases

Husbands, in *The Rape of the Lock* as in Restoration comedy, are blessed with scant respect. They are bedded in casual disorder with the other domestic pets: for instance, in the description of Belinda's outcry at the fateful moment:

> Not louder Shrieks to pitying Heav'n are cast,
> When Husbands or when Lap-dogs breathe their last,
> Or when rich *China* Vessels, fal'n from high,
> In glittring Dust and painted Fragments lie! (iii. 157–60)

The shrieks over a dead husband would be, we may think, a deal more perfunctory than those over the other treasures.

To the domestic playthings and ornaments of the belle's *ménage*, Pope gives an ironic prominence, in inverse proportion to their value in any sensible scale of importance. Thalestris' catalogue of disasters is an absurd tumble of discrepant items, though she *intends* a compliment to the less fair sex:

Sooner let Earth, Air, Sea, to *Chaos* fall,
Men, Monkies, Lap-dogs, Parrots, perish all! (iv. 119–20)

To Ariel, the possible fall of Belinda's lap-dog, Shock, is an unthinkable calamity; and Belinda herself, grieving for the snatched lock, recalls the unregarded portents of the morning—'*Poll* sate mute, and *Shock* was most Unkind!' (iv. 164).

Whether presented as alternatives or as items in enumeration, the pets and vases cannot be kept separate from the other things in their immediate context; in fact, Pope compels the mind to try to hold them all together at once, as the belles contrive to do with so little effort. Thalestris, ranking men as low (we would think) as monkeys and lap-dogs, is actually up-grading them. In

Now Lapdogs give themselves the rowzing Shake,
And sleepless Lovers, just at Twelve, awake (i. 15–16)

there is a double insinuation—that lovers are very like lap-dogs, and that lap-dogs are thought as important as lovers, to be dandled with equal fondness and condescension. In Ariel's series of (he takes it) equal alternatives, the loss of maidenhead and the breaking of frail china are juxtaposed: this insinuates that in the belle's eyes the two calamities are on a par, and the vase's qualities are transferred to the alternative item. This transference all but establishes china as a symbol for maidenhood. When it is brought in to complete the evocation of Belinda's grief for the vanished curl—

when rich *China* Vessels, fal'n from high,
In glittring Dust and painted Fragments lie!

we sense mainly the absurdity of taking the vases so seriously, but also, through the symbol, the nature of the insult that has been offered. The damage cannot be undone: beauty and chastity are brittle. But in the Cave of Spleen this symbol, like so much else, meets its grosser counterpart: 'Here sighs a Jar' (iv. 52).

The lock and the sun

Like many other things in the poem, the fateful curls are touched with brilliance and divinity. They are described as 'radiant' and 'shining', and the Baron swears by them. With her hair alone, Belinda can

accomplish the enslavement, even the destruction, of mankind, drawing
men like tickled trout:

> With hairy Sprindges we the Birds betray,
> Slight Lines of Hair surprize the Finny Prey,
> Fair Tresses Man's Imperial Race insnare,
> And Beauty draws us with a single Hair. (ii. 25–8)

Here, Pope pushes hyperbole and sententious reflection to the verge of
ridicule, in a context, moreover, that invites a qualified response: before
these lines, we have been watching Belinda at the exercise of her powers,
and we are about to witness the Baron staging his own private love-
entangled scene. The lock's transcendent beauty and power, Pope insinuates, is partly another make-believe in the eyes of Belinda's vanity
and the Baron's rapacity.

But the fiction of the sacred lock also delights Pope. He taps a reser-
voir of conceit, extravagant compliment and elegant nothings that is
both shallow and deep: after all, a *cliché* has attracted a lot of users in its
day. It is not wholly absurd for Belinda to denounce the rape as sac-
rilege, or to take the loss of the curls as the first stage in the compromise
of innocence and trust:

> The Sister-Lock now sits uncouth, alone,
> And in its Fellow's Fate foresees its own;
> Uncurl'd it hangs, the fatal Sheers demands;
> And tempts once more thy sacrilegious Hands. (iv. 171–4)

Yet her very next couplet exposes her, out of her own mouth, to the
compromising implication that she would have preferred any other out-
rage or intimacy to one so public:

> Oh hadst thou, Cruel! been content to seize
> Hairs less in sight, or any Hairs but these!

Fittingly, the lock is glorified as a new star, in the last of the poem's
many metamorphoses. Once again, Pope compels a double response.
There are the self-conscious, rather too grand, literary allusions—'So
Rome's great Founder to the Heav'ns withdrew'—and the mundane,
over-topical corrective—the Mall, Rosamunda's lake and the astrologer
Partridge peering, in another metamorphosis, 'thro' *Galilæo*'s Eyes'.
In the teeth of this series of discrepancies the last paragraph earns its
genuine resonance. That it does so is partly owing to Pope's use of the

sun image, which has been, in varying ways, associated with Belinda throughout. It woke her, as its feared rival, at the opening of the poem, and shone through her day, benign or ominous as appropriate. In the end, the rise of the new star coincides with a sunset, the metaphorical decline of Belinda's beauty and even her death. Fragile as precious china, transient as daylight, her natural element, Belinda's beauty is given its fitting homage, in a confluence of romantic exaggeration and epic sonority:

> For, after all the Murders of your Eye,
> When, after Millions slain, your self shall die . . . (v. 145–6)

5. *Positive Capability*

I was able to plead that my postulates, my animating presences, were all, to their great enrichment, their intensification of value, ironic; the strength of applied irony being surely in the sincerities, the lucidities, the utilities that stand behind it. . . . It implies and projects the possible other case, the case rich and edifying where the actuality is pretentious and vain. So it plays its lamp; so, essentially, it carries that smokeless flame, which makes clear, with all the rest, the good cause that guides it.

Henry James, Preface to 'The Lesson of the Master'

The 'animating presences' of the classical tradition inform Pope's entire output as a poet, influencing it in ways beyond number, pervasive and specific, direct and oblique, stabilising and distancing the satirist's material. What might merely have frayed the nerve-ends of his sensibility is kept in check, to be viewed with a measure of dispassion, shaped and measured in his confidence of the tradition's moral authority and artistic precedence, and governed by a whole system of checks and balances by means of which the impulse to deride and retaliate is geared to the exacting demands of *decorum* and restraint. In the light of 'the sincerities, the lucidities, the utilities' of the classics, no manifestation of the opposite spirit need be either too trivial to cast a shadow or too over-setting to be looked at calmly—the *in*sincerities, greater and less, of Atticus and Belinda; the moral muddle of Thalestris and, worse, Lord Timon; the *in*utility of the Baron's postures and, appallingly, Atossa's hysterical anger.

Pope's growth as a poet is not, of course, to be measured simply in terms of a developing mastery of the heroic couplet. To say this is not to disparage the 'technical' aspect of his achievement. But however much his poetry compels *awareness* of its skills, Pope in the long run defies discussion in terms of mere verse technique; indeed, these terms were for long the faint praise used to damn him as an accomplished metronome. The metrical skills *are* vital: fastidious without seeming laboured, dexterous with a seemingly nonchalant sureness of touch. But in talking of Pope's couplets at their best, we should think not only of his *fitting* material *into* the metrical form but also of an intimate formative interplay between the two, each reacting upon the other. The couplet can be as intimately tied, and as subtly responsive, to a creative intelligence, as forms apparently much 'freer', like mature Shakespearian blank verse. We have a sense, certainly, of an *anterior* struggle to achieve compression and bite, the process of 'turning' a couplet which Pope never tired of; but there is also the sense of a continuing tension between the matched components, in the line, the couplet, the paragraph and the whole poem.

In terms of some such continuing tension Pope's development may perhaps be best described. It is, of course, reflected in—indeed, it demands—a growing range and refinement of skills. But it is primarily a growing ability to admit into the poetry, and explore in it, more and more details of the contingent world immediately present to Pope's consciousness—topicalities, proper names, events; the sordid, prosaic, insignificant—without relaxing the positive artistic and moral command which is derived from his sense of the 'possible other case':

> Pretty! in Amber to observe the Forms
> Of Hairs, or Straws, or Dirt, or Grubs, or Worms!
> The Things, we know, are neither rich nor rare,
> But wonder how the Devil they got there![1]

The Dunciad, for instance, is packed with trivialities, obscenities, fragments and snippets. But they are all, so to speak, caught in the amber of the other possibility—the possibility of dignity, significance, coherence. The power to open his poetry to the pressures of his environment, down to the merest detail and the most personal distaste, and to accomplish this without compromising the standards against which they can be judged, is more than an artistic resourcefulness. It is, to adapt Keats's phrase, Pope's *positive capability*: a firm moral and artistic sense coping

[1] Prologue to the *Satires*, 169–72.

with the findings, ugly and beautiful alike, of a fine, vulnerable sen-
sitiveness. *The Rape of the Lock* is much less cluttered with detail than
The Dunciad—it is not to its purpose to yield so much to the pressure of
the squalid or the trivial. But it exhibits, none the less, the working of
this capability of Pope's.

It is no longer unreasonable, nor unfashionable, to speak of this as an
imaginative power. Professor Mack, defining mock-heroic as 'the
metaphor of tone', comments:

> By its means, without the use of overt imagery at all, opposite and
> discordant qualities may be locked together in 'a balance or reconcile-
> ment of sameness with difference, of the general with the concrete,
> the idea with the image, the individual with the representative, the
> sense of novelty and freshness with old and familiar objects'—the
> mock-heroic seems made on purpose to fit this definition of
> Coleridge's of the power of imagination.[1]

To apply Coleridge's definition to an Augustan poet would once have
seemed a gross miscalculation: Pope's reputation in Romantic criticism
tended to be that of one prosaically arid of imaginative power. But it
is now possible to read, for instance, of 'the whirlwind of metaphorical
activity going on in *The Rape of the Lock*'[2] without suspecting an abuse
of the term 'metaphor'. Indeed, it is conceivable that critics of Pope
may come to pay attention to the 'metaphorical density' of his poetry
at the expense of his wit. To emphasise the play of wit in his poetry is
not to take issue with the critics just quoted; nor is it to retreat towards
the Arnoldian distinction between 'genuine poetry . . . conceived and
composed in the soul' and the superficial poetry of 'ratiocination,
antithesis, ingenious turns and conceits'.[3] It is, rather, to remind our-
selves of the proximity between Coleridge's definition of imagination
and one of Johnson's definitions of wit. Johnson praised *The Rape of the
Lock* in terms very close to the last item in Coleridge's definition: 'new
things are made familiar, and familiar things are made new'.[4] His
definition of one kind of wit closely anticipates Coleridge:

> a kind of *discordia concors*; a combination of dissimilar images, or dis-
> covery of occult resemblances in things apparently unlike.[5]

[1] Mack, p. 36.   [2] Parkin, p. 115.
[3] *Essays in Criticism*, ed. 1938, Second Series, p. 56.
[4] *Lives*, III. 233. See also p. 29 above.
[5] *Lives*, I. 20.

This wit he found displayed to excess in the metaphysical poets, in whom

> The most heterogeneous ideas are yoked by violence together; nature and art are ransacked for illustrations, comparisons, and allusions.[1]

Each of these statements applies readily to *The Rape*, but the phrase 'yoked by violence' is crucial. Certainly the poem brings into close proximity 'opposite and discordant qualities'; but only rarely does it entirely balance or reconcile them, and then precariously. We are almost always aware of the violence, the distortion, that has accompanied the process of bringing them together—or, in other words, the tension between the matched components in the metaphor. This tension is, of course, vital to the irony: to be aware of it is to read the ironic implications. Indeed, the term 'conceit' seems to fit mock-heroic best of all. It is a species of metaphor, but one whose components, often startlingly incongruous, are never quite locked together; and in it we expect, on account of its association with the metaphysical poets, the interplay of imagination and wit.

The Rape of the Lock is, finally, the achievement of a spirited imaginative intelligence. To marshal a host of literary allusions, at varying levels of suppression, from the blatantly overt to the secretive; to carry the mimicry of epic to the furthest lengths, from major items of epic structure down to niceties of heroic idiom and tone; to maintain a firm discrimination between the admirable and the trashy in contemporary society, unmasking hypocrisy and pretentiousness: such activities engage the intelligence, as well ours as Pope's. But there is a sustained effort of wit and imagination behind those other aspects of the poem which are less readily found in other mock-heroic, other satire: the startling discovery of aptness and congruence, bridging the discrepancy between heroic and contemporary worlds; the continuous doubleness of apprehension, by which the bathetic can yield poignancy, the mock-portentous can function genuinely, the trivial can seem significant; and not least, Pope's grasp of the poem's developing identity, as it more than doubled its length in the major revision of 1714, and later, as an opening was made for Clarissa's speech, itself a climax in the witty, imaginative balancing of world against world.

[1] *Lives*, I. 20.

Bibliography

list below books and articles referred to in the text, giving the footnote abbreviations on the left.

Aeneid   Dryden's translation, ed. James Kinsley, *The Poems of John Dryden*, Oxford, 1958, vol. iv.

Brower   R. A. Brower, *Alexander Pope: The Poetry of Allusion*, Oxford, 1959.

Correspondence *The Correspondence of Alexander Pope*, ed. G. Sherburn, Oxford, 1956.

Dacier   Mme Dacier, *The Iliad of Homer, With Notes*, trans. Ozell, London, 1712.

Dennis   John Dennis, *The Critical Works*, ed. E. N. Hooker, Baltimore, 1939–43 (2 vols.).

Iliad   Pope's translation, London, 1715–20 (6 vols.). References to Pope's text are by book and line; those to his editorial material by volume and page.

Knight   Douglas Knight, *Pope and the Heroic Tradition*, Yale, 1951.

Lives   Samuel Johnson, *Lives of the Poets*, ed. G. B. Hill, Oxford, 1905.

Mack   Maynard Mack, ' "Wit and Poetry and Pope" ': Some Observations on his Imagery', in *Pope and his Contemporaries*, ed. J. L. Clifford and L. A. Landa, Oxford, 1949, p. 20.

Odyssey   Pope's translation, London, 1725–6 (5 vols.). References to volume and page.

Parkin   Rebecca Price Parkin, *The Poetic Workmanship of Alexander Pope*, Minnesota, 1955.

Rapin   René Rapin, *Observations on the Poems of Homer and Virgil*, trans. J. Davies, London, 1672.

Reichard   Hugo M. Reichard, 'The Love Affair in Pope's *Rape of the Lock*', *P.M.L.A.*, Sept. 1954, vol. lxix, p. 887.

Spence   Joseph Spence, *Observations, Anecdotes, and Characters of Books and Men*, ed. 1820.

The Twickenham text of Pope's poetry is used for quotations throughout, except in the case of the Homer translations and those poems which have yet to appear in this edition.

Selective Index